Access your online resources

Cultural Inclusion for Young People with SEND is accompanied by a number of printable online materials, designed to ensure this resource best supports your professional needs.

Activate your online resources:

Go to www.routledge.com/cw/morrow and click on the cover of this book.

Click the 'Sign in or Request Access' button and follow the instructions in order to access the resources.

Ultimately, cultural inclusion is an essential piece of the jigsaw for ensuring that all children and young people have the opportunity to reach their full potential. Paul has brought the reality of this to life through this book. It's now time for all of us to play our part in building a culturally rich and more inclusive world.

Professor Adam Boddison, *Visiting Professor of Education,*
University of Wolverhampton

Cultural Inclusion for Young People with SEND

This practical book offers a multifaceted view of cultural inclusion from the perspective of special educational needs and disabilities (SEND).

It provides a road map for teachers to ensure increased participation in arts and culture for children and young people with SEND, defining a series of characteristics for good practice. Chapters explore spaces as diverse as galleries, museums, theatres, and performance venues and include a variety of case studies, highlighting the experiences of young people and the organisations who partner with schools.

Cultural Inclusion for Young People with SEND offers a compelling call to action and is an essential resource for those who have the power to improve and support the development of future provision for children with SEND.

Paul Morrow is Lead Practitioner of the Creative Arts at Westminster Special Schools and a practising artist. Paul founded the West London Inclusive Arts Festival, a festival funded by the John Lyon's Charity involving six special needs schools and six cultural partners. He is also the co-author of the Cultural Inclusion Manifesto.

Other titles published in association with the National Association for Special Educational Needs (nasen):

Cultural Inclusion for Young People with SEND

Practical Strategies for Meaningful Inclusion in Arts and Culture

Paul Morrow

Routledge
Taylor & Francis Group

LONDON AND NEW YORK

Designed cover image: Image courtesy of College Park School

First published 2023
by Routledge
4 Park Square, Milton Park, Abingdon, Oxon OX14 4RN

and by Routledge
605 Third Avenue, New York, NY 10158

Routledge is an imprint of the Taylor & Francis Group, an informa business

© 2023 Paul Morrow

The right of Paul Morrow to be identified as author of this work has been asserted in accordance with sections 77 and 78 of the Copyright, Designs and Patents Act 1988.

British Library Cataloguing-in-Publication Data
A catalogue record for this book is available from the British Library

Library of Congress Cataloging-in-Publication Data
Names: Morrow, Paul, author.
Title: Cultural inclusion for young people with SEND : practical strategies for meaningful inclusion in arts and culture / Paul Morrow.
Description: Abingdon, Oxon ; New York, NY : Routledge, 2023. | Series: Nasen spotlight ; Volume 44 | Includes index.
Identifiers: LCCN 2022030811 (print) | LCCN 2022030812 (ebook) | ISBN 9780367641252 (hardback) | ISBN 9780367641238 (paperback) | ISBN 9781003122258 (ebook)
Subjects: LCSH: Inclusive education. | People with disabilities and the arts. | Learning disabled children—Education. | Students with disabilities—Education. | Multicultural education.
Classification: LCC LC1200 .M846 2023 (print) | LCC LC1200 (ebook) | DDC 371.9/046—dc23/eng/20220713
LC record available at https://lccn.loc. gov/2022030811
LC ebook record available at https://lccn.loc.gov/2022030812

ISBN: 978-0-367-64125-2 (hbk)
ISBN: 978-0-367-64123-8 (pbk)
ISBN: 978-1-003-12225-8 (ebk)

DOI: 10.4324/9781003122258

Access the companion website: www.routledge.com/cw/morrow

Contents

Acknowledgements

I would like to thank Professor Adam Boddison for asking me to write the book. I would also like to thank Anita Kerwin-Nye for her mentorship and her ongoing support for this work. I would also like to thank Rachael Christophides for her support with the structure and for being a constant sounding board.

I would also like to thank Andrew Miller and Dr Claire Penketh of Liverpool Hope University for informing my thinking.

I would like to thank the parents who contributed to the book, Stephen Unwin, April Li, Claire Madge, and Lisha Rooney.

I would also like to thank Open City and Sarah Philips and the musician Luke Crookes and the artist Marc Woodhead.

I would like to thank Sarah Archdeacon and DJ of Corali Dance Company, Sheryll Catto and Charlotte Hollinshead of ActionSpace, Jodi-Alissa Bickerton of Graeae Theatre Company, Jennifer Gilbert of the Jennifer Lauren Gallery, and Douglas Noble and Carien Meijer of Drake Music.

I would also like to thank Ruth Boley and Dwayne Rose of the Maritime Museum, and the author Karin Littlewood and Amy Chang and Dorothée Perin of the Wallace Collection.

I would like to thank Amy Powell and Beth Warnock of the English National Opera, Jess Thom of Touretteshero, and Aymeline Bel and Elise Robinson of Queensmill School.

And lastly all my colleagues at my home school, Westminster Special Schools, especially Tatjana Zeljic and Claire Shepherd for their constant support and interest in this work.

Foreword

When I first met Paul, his passion for inclusion and the arts was abundantly obvious. With a foot in both worlds, he had unique insights into how inclusion could support culture and how culture could support inclusion. The argument for cultural inclusion was compelling from the outset and the benefits were clear, but there was a problem. An increasingly complex cultural and educational landscape was preventing this important work from coming to fruition. Those engaged with cultural inclusion were reaping the rewards, but the wider reach and potential impact was yet to be realised. This book is one of the vehicles that can help cultural inclusion reach the audience it deserves.

Reading Paul's book, I am struck by how effective he has been in taking a complicated set of ideas and communicating them so clearly to multiple audiences. For example, the book explicitly makes the case for inclusion in cultural settings as well as for culturally inclusive curricula in schools. Schools and cultural settings may not always have the same priorities, but complementarity can be built around cultural inclusion. Paul also interweaves research, policy and practice in a way that is designed to build capacity and momentum for cultural inclusion. I have no doubt that the practical advice and templates will be a valuable resource for those seeking to implement cultural inclusion.

Cultural inclusion is about ensuring that everybody has access to heritage, culture and the arts. Children and young people with SEND (special educational needs and/or disabilities) are already too often marginalised in society. This amplifies the importance of cultural inclusion for children and young people with SEND; the absence of cultural inclusion exacerbates division, but its presence is a catalyst for inclusion more generally.

Similarly, the diversity of the arts world has a particular synergy with the diversity and creativity of children who think differently and see the world differently. Therefore, cultural inclusion is about more than making sure that children and young people with SEND do not miss out on having arts, culture and heritage in their lives. It is also about ensuring that we as a society do not miss out on their talent and their creativity. Paul captures the essence of this principle throughout the book.

Ultimately, cultural inclusion is an essential piece of the jigsaw for ensuring that all children and young people have the opportunity to reach their full potential. Paul has brought the reality of this to life through this book. It's now time for all of us to play our part in building a culturally rich and more inclusive world.

Professor Adam Boddison
Visiting Professor of Education, University of Wolverhampton

1   Introduction

The need for cultural inclusion

This book came about due to a number of factors, two of which were my work as an educator in the space of arts, culture, and inclusion and also as a response to co-authoring the Cultural Inclusion Manifesto.

The Cultural Inclusion Manifesto

The Cultural Inclusion Manifesto was developed in 2018 as a response to the lack of access to artistic and cultural opportunities for disabled children and young people. Many SEND (special educational needs and/or disabilities) and arts and culture organisations had been setting a path towards greater inclusion of young people with disabilities in arts and culture for some time, but final inspiration for the Manifesto was the West London Inclusive Arts Festival. Supported by John Lyon's Charity, four special schools worked alongside two cultural partners – the Wallace Collection and the Lyric Theatre in Hammersmith – to deliver high-quality cultural and arts events with inclusion and inclusive practice at their core.

Guiding set of principles

It soon became clear that we needed a starting point, a guiding set of principles. This is where the Cultural Inclusion Manifesto started to take form. It outlines a vision of future partnership working and greater connectivity. It looks to be a space to guide, support, and be a bank of best practice to support the ongoing drive towards real inclusion.

The need for greater connectivity

Working within this space demonstrated the power of arts and culture and their transformative qualities for young people with SEND. During this time, I also conceived the West London Inclusive Arts Festival, a festival that I led for several years and which gave me some insights into partnership working across schools, cultural organisations, and families.

Through this work I discovered that equity in access wasn't always the common experience for a number of young people with SEND. This was due in part to a number of issues, in some cases a lack of know-how within this space, for others a lack of connection into this space. As an educationalist working in this field, I was lucky to work with a number of organisations, schools, galleries, museums, and families to increase inclusion.

The need for material in this space

There is very little material that explores the concept of inclusion within the space of arts, culture, and inclusion for young people who have learning needs and for those with a diagnosis of a hearing impairment, disability, or neurodivergence that is across sector. The purpose of this book is to take a broad view of this space, to capture and articulate inclusion by speaking to those people who both inhabit and influence this space: schools, cultural organisations, and disabled-led and disabled-focus cultural organisations.

Through this journey I learnt more about how these relationships can be both facilitated and brokered, how to support inclusion, and how to articulate this in relation to education policy and practice and in the classroom in relationship to both pedagogy and curriculum design. It also offers guidance on fundraising to schools and how to demonstrate impact institutionally and for students in terms of inclusive assessment approaches.

This chapter will introduce you to some of the themes and concepts that are used to explore this space. These ideas will be referred to throughout the book as a means to best understand and explain inclusion and inclusive practice.

DOI: 10.4324/9781003122258-1

The multifaceted view

This book importantly acknowledges that progress needs to take place across a number of spaces for a sustained cultural change. For this to happen, inclusion will be explored through both policy and practice. It will define inclusion in a wide range of settings, including galleries, museums, and places of performance. It will view these spaces from the perspective of disabled people. It will consider how young people with special educational needs are both producing and consuming arts and culture. It will also take the position that access to arts and culture is a **fundamental human right** and not a privilege.

Case studies and practical advice

The purposes of this book are to effect change, to offer practical advice and guidance. As inclusion is central to this book, it will use a qualitative assessment approach in capturing this.

Qualitative assessment is an approach to assessment which chimes with the ethos of inclusion. It gives useful insights on how to make progress and most importantly describes how and in what way inclusion was realised and experienced by those involved. To achieve this chapters will use a combination of case studies and/or interviews. Through this process I will both articulate and determine qualities that can be described as both the characteristics and signifiers of inclusion and inclusive practice. These can then be distilled into **practical guidance and advice**. To support this, I will also develop and identify appropriate resources that can be used to support cultural inclusion.

Where are we now?

The current context, damning statistics

Delving deeper into this space reveals worrying statistics that confirm that high-quality access and inclusion into arts and culture is not the common experience.

Statistics from the **Department for Culture, Media and Sport (DCMS)** demonstrate that:

- There is a significant difference between the proportion of children with and without a limiting disability who had visited a heritage site in the 5–10 age bracket (**53.1%** and **71.5%** respectively)
- Nondisabled children and young people aged 11–15 are **twice** as likely to visit a museum with their school than their disabled peers are

Similarly, research by the **Arts Council** identified the barriers that exist for disabled children and young people:

- **Physical access** – **42%** of venues in one study reported that visually impaired people could access little of their collections (Shape Arts 2013)
- **Accessible information** – **nearly half** of learning-disabled young people rely on parents, carers, or schools for information about events and activities (Mencap 2009)
- **Poor accessibility on arts websites** – including buying tickets for cultural events (Consilium 2014)
- **Transport** – availability, accessibility, practicality, and cost
- **Support to attend arts** – especially outside of school hours (Mencap 2009)
- **Concerns from disabled people** – most learning-disabled young people prefer inclusive sessions but have concerns about harassment and whether they would 'fit in' or be welcome. Making clear the level and pace of activity so people can judge whether it would be right for them is also important (Mencap 2009)
- The scope of the challenge is confirmed in the recently released **London Mayor's Cultural Strategy** which points out that **almost a third** of UK museums provide no access information on their websites for disabled people planning a visit, and many theatres fail to reach audiences with disabilities

Cultural values

Research conducted by Warwick University reveals that there has been a significant decline in the number of state schools offering arts subjects taught by specialist teachers. The report, the **Warwick Commission on the Future of Cultural Values**, found that between 2003 and 2013 there was a **50%** drop in general certificate of secondary education (GCSE) entries for design and technology, **23%** for drama, and **25%** for other craft-related subjects. Additionally, research from the **Education Policy Institute** has shown a decline in the proportion of pupils taking at least one arts subject at GCSE level. In 2016 it reached **53.5%**, the lowest level for a decade.

The Warwick Commission concluded that it is also essential to ensure that we are focusing on the current and future needs of the cultural and creative industries as well as the broader need for innovation and growth in the UK.

John Kampfner, from the **Creative Industries Federation**, said it was worrying that some schools were reporting that art subjects were now seen as softer options:

> Arts provision should also be seen as a core subject. There's nothing soft about subjects that create the talent that creates the fastest growing sector of our economy.

Mental health and wellbeing

In addition to the educational value of inclusion and participation in the arts, and the contribution it makes to preparing our children and young people to meet the future needs of the UK economy, it also has an enormous impact on health and wellbeing. **The London Mayor's Cultural Strategy** notes:

> There is mounting evidence . . . that creativity and the arts make a significant difference to people's physical and mental health and wellbeing. Culture can play a role within clinical settings and in the wider community. It can help people maintain good health and wellbeing or recover from illness.

The strategy refers to an arts-on-prescription project which led to a **37%** drop-in GP consultation rates and a **27%** reduction in hospital admissions. This was estimated to save the National Health Service (NHS) £216 per patient.

The link between participation in the arts and improved health outcomes has long been recognised. Over a decade ago research conducted by the **Department of Health** found that:

* Arts and health are, and should be firmly recognised as being, integral to health, healthcare provision, and healthcare environments, including supporting staff
* Arts and health initiatives are delivering real and measurable benefits across a wide range of priority areas for health and can enable the Department of Health and NHS to contribute to key wider government initiatives
* There is a wealth of good practice and a substantial evidence base

More recently a review of the impact of arts on society, commissioned by the **Arts Council**, found that:

* Those who attended a cultural place or event in the previous 12 months were almost **60%** more likely to report good health compared to those that had not
* Theatre goers were almost **25%** more likely to report good health
* There is clear evidence that a higher frequency of engagement with arts and culture is generally associated with a higher level of subjective wellbeing
* Engagement in structured arts and culture improves the cognitive abilities of children and young people
* The use of arts, when delivered effectively, has the power to facilitate social interaction as well as ensuring that those in receipt of social care can pursue creative interests
* Participation in dance has significant benefits for reducing loneliness and alleviating depression and anxiety for people in social care environments

Last year the **All-Party Parliamentary Group on Arts, Health and Wellbeing** conducted a review of the available evidence that arts and culture make an enormous contribution to improving health outcomes. They concluded:

> It is time to recognise the powerful contribution the arts can make to health and wellbeing. There are now many examples and much evidence of the beneficial impact they can have.

Their report outlined three key messages:

* The arts can help keep us well, aid our recovery, and support longer lives better lived.
* The arts can help meet major challenges facing health and social care: ageing, long-term conditions, loneliness, and mental health.
* The arts can help save money in the health service and social care.

These stats paint a picture of an area of both great value and impact in the broadest holistic manner, but also one that isn't equitable.

It might be useful to quote these statistics when building a case for support for a project.

Key concepts in inclusion

Social model of disability

This book applies the social model of disability, a model which was developed in the 1960s and 70s as part of the growing civil rights movements that were gaining traction at that time. The social model of disability describes a way of thinking and conceptualising inclusion.

The social model of disability identifies and pathologises those structures that are barriers to inclusion within society and its systems and structures and **not the individual**. These barriers can be systemic barriers which are spread throughout society. They can be attitudinal, and based on stereotypes and preconceptions. The model is one that supports social change in the sense that it not only identifies barriers, it also offers up possible solutions to them.

The barriers that the social model of disability identifies can lead to social exclusion and affect how people are perceived and valued. Within this model it is worth noting that it separates out the impairment – cognitive, sensory, or physical – from the disability. The disability is the social consequence and impact that the impairment leads to and is a social construct of disability. This book will look at how some of these barriers have been removed and what the practical learning is, and how it can be used to support other individuals and organisations.

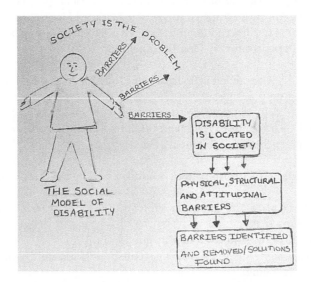

Image 1.1 Illustration of the social model of disability by Paul Morrow

The medical model of disability

The social model of disability is in opposition to the medical model of disability which locates the barriers within the individual. Here the solution is for the individual to change or be modified so that they can access society; within this model the individual would have increased societal value. This model also corresponds with the notion of normalcy, an idea that is explored later in this chapter.

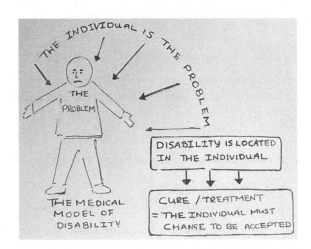

Image 1.2 Illustration of the medical model of disability by Paul Morrow

There is no agreed definition of inclusion

It is worth noting that there is no agreed definition of inclusion; this concept will be explored further throughout the chapter.

What does inclusion look like?

Arts and culture as a mirror of society

Arts and culture are the mirror of society. They reflect our history and our values and the stories and narratives that give our society form and shape. Arts and culture can also be the space and place for change. Additionally, they can be a space for change and dialogue – dialogue that can agitate, question, and challenge – and a space for progression. This book seeks to broaden this dialogue, to be a practical support across this space to further cultural inclusion for young people with learning needs and those with a diagnosis of disability.

Social exclusion

A report published by Levitas et al. (2007:9) defined social exclusion as:

> A complex and multi-dimensional process. It involves the lack or denial of resources, rights, goods and services, and the inability to participate in the normal relationships and activities, available to the majority of people in a society, whether in economic, social, cultural or political arenas.

The report goes on further to illustrate how this:

> affects both the quality of life of individuals and the equity and cohesion of society as a whole.

This underlines the importance of how disabled people and disabilities are portrayed within arts and culture and how the value that this generates impacts on the lives of disabled people within wider society. It also highlights the importance of this conversation and the moral duty that we have to challenge the structures, systems, and attitude that can lead to social exclusion.

Labelling

The notion and concept of labelling can be problematic. Inclusive labelling is a sign-posting exercise that can give you some understanding of the impairment that people have and what barriers it could lead to. It is important to note that you should label only if it is empowering and enabling, and that you should always acknowledge the person first and the impairment second. The impairment does not define a person.

Normalcy

The concept and idea of normalcy is inextricably linked to the notion of disabilities. The idea of normal is relational to the idea of what could be described as abnormal: the language here locates impairments – physical, cognitive, and sensory – within a deficit model. The idea is a social construct that has been promoted and embedded in society for a long time and is the dominant model. The model of normalcy refers to the idea of what is seen as 'normal', and this has then informed systems and structures in society. This concept of normalcy promotes a societal view that all in society are to correspond to and be measured by. Society was largely designed in relation to this idea, and those who were different were seen as being in deficit. This located the deficit within the individual and corresponds with the medical model of disability: 'fixing' the individual so that they can better fit in with society. The model is one that oppresses and defines differences as a negative.

Othering

The idea of the other, again like the notion of normalcy, describes an individual or a group of individuals as different, separate from another group. The term usually corresponds with how individuals or groups of people are perceived and treated as different; again, this sits within a model of deficit and hierarchy.

Ableism

Ableism is the term that describes the prejudice and discrimination experienced by people with disabilities or people who are perceived to have disabilities. Ableism also refers to the assumptions that are made and imposed upon this group. It also refers to the stereotypes and their corresponding abilities and skills that are assigned or denied as a consequence.

Social role valorisation and normalisation

Social role valorisation (SRV) is a model that acknowledges the power of how people are portrayed and its subsequent impact on the value that society locates within that individual. SRV was developed as a response to the notion of normalisation and how those that were portrayed differently could be seen as having a lower societal value, which would subsequently lead to having less access and fewer opportunities across a number of spaces. This would also directly impact on their access to health care, wellbeing, and outcomes. This model relates directly to the notion of **normalisation**. Wolfensberger (1980) developed the concept of SRV. Its purpose was to support the development and maintenance of roles specifically for those who were at the greatest risk of having their roles devalued in society.

Wolfensberger describes how SRV was

> Developed and defined as the use of culturally typical or valued means to support people at risk of devaluation to have the same living conditions and be supported in their experiences, behaviour, status, and reputation so that it is at least the same as the average citizen.
>
> (Wolfensberger, 1980)

Making the unseen seen

Within SRV there are ten themes that explore the notion of societal value. One of these themes relates directly on how people are portrayed. This is defined as 'Positive social image, because imagery both shapes and reflects a person's social roles and conveys to observers what social roles a perceived party holds'. The model acknowledges and reflects the power that imagery holds in society. Wolfensberger's model highlights the importance of imagery generated through cultural production in shaping society's expectations and attitudes of people, but most importantly it also acknowledges how much of this is accepted unconsciously. The model acknowledges that social constructs inherent in society can lead to devaluation and draws attention to these constructs. The importance of societal value and how it is constructed and the subsequent impact on that person's quality of life demonstrate how social exclusion can occur. SRV is a model that is used widely in the development of public policy.

Hope for the future

The book explores how and in what way inclusive practices present, through an inclusive arts festival, considering how its design and delivery were informed by inclusion. It looks at a number of case studies. It unpacks the characteristics of anti-ableist pedagogy to the co-production of learning resources, trips, and outreach sessions in collaboration with the Wallace Collection and the Maritime Museum. It looks at contemporary art and how some of its practices align with inclusive pedagogy. It also talks to parents to hear of their first-hand experiences of this space. It has been a joy to learn about the many aspects of this wide topic through researching for the book, and I hope that you enjoy this book as much as I enjoyed researching and writing it.

References

Levitas, R., Pantazis, C., Fahmy, E., Gordon, D., Lloyd, E. and Patsios, D. (2007) *The multi-Dimensional Analysis of Social Exclusion*. Bristol: Department of Sociology and School for Social Policy Townsend Centre for the International Study of Poverty and Bristol Institute for Public Affairs, University of Bristol.

Wolfensberger, W. (1980) The definition of normalization: Update, problems, disagreements and misunderstandings. In Fylnn, R.J. and Nitsch, K.E. (eds.), *Normalization, Social Integration and Community Services*, pp. 71–115. Baltimore: University Park Press.

2 What does inclusion look like?

Inclusion needs to be constantly explored and evaluated using practical experience to ensure that it continues to evolve to meet the emerging needs of schools, cultural organisations, young people, and their families. The more that inclusion is discussed the greater our knowledge and understanding of inclusion becomes and our understanding of its principles and application to real life.

Inclusion within the lived experience

Inclusion is anchored within the lived experience and, as such, it is defined by the spaces in which it takes place and the individuals within these spaces. For this reason, the book will explore inclusivity from a point of equity of access, use real case studies to examine how it has been defined, and illustrate to increase our understanding of what best practice looks like in specific environments.

What this chapter will explore

This chapter will identify some of the practical challenges that inclusion presents and gives specific examples, such as a focus on process over product. It looks at the idea of co-production and of anticipating need, but also of being flexible and adaptive. It also considers how relationships are central to promoting inclusion and inclusive practice. This will be of real practical use to the reader in their journey towards inclusion.

This chapter discusses some of the ways in which inclusion is developed and the processes that support it. It looks at some fundamental elements to inclusive practice that both schools and cultural organisations can use to articulate how and which way they are being inclusive. Firstly, the chapter asks, what does inclusion look like? It then breaks this down, exploring some of its constituent parts for greater understanding.

How to use this chapter

Practical guidance

The practical guidance at the end of this chapter looks at how you can use evaluation tools and case studies that demonstrate the positive impact of inclusion for a number of audiences, such as funders and in school settings, how this can both denote impact and support pedagogy.

What does inclusion look like in cultural settings?

The question of what inclusion looks like is dependent on a number of factors. Inclusion can be described as an ethos, an approach and a commitment to working in the spirit of inclusion – these principles both support and signify inclusion. As mentioned previously there is no agreed definition of inclusion, but for the purpose of this book I will develop a working definition of inclusion. There are what can be described as characteristics of inclusion, and these are what we will explore in this chapter to guide your understanding of inclusion and its application to a range of settings.

Words in boxes

You will notice that throughout this chapter certain words are bold and in boxes. These words are those that are associated with inclusion and will help you in your understanding, articulation, and application of inclusion within your setting.

DOI: 10.4324/9781003122258-2

Developing a working definition of inclusion

Inclusion is a movement that is not only applicable in educational settings but is now impacting in a broader societal manner. As mentioned previously, reaching a general description of inclusion is a possibility, but its application will be different based on specific factors such as location, institution, and most importantly the individuals that inclusion is applied to.

> Inclusive education, while initially focusing on providing for students with disabilities in mainstream schools, now encompasses a much broader definition that refers to all children that historically have been marginalised from meaningful education.
>
> (Forlin, 2010:4)

Inclusion is the mechanism and process by which these groups are included.

Anchoring inclusion in your practices

Task

- Consider what inclusion means to you. How would you describe it?
- Can you give an example of how and in what way you, or the organisation that you work in, is inclusive?

An amorphous term

Inclusion is an amorphous term that can mean different things in different settings. This is due in part to there being no fixed definition either nationally or internationally.

The use of the term inclusion was first deployed by the International League of Societies for Persons with Mental Handicap (ILSMH). The organisation announced that it was changing its name to Inclusion International in 1996: 'This new name expresses a hope for the future. It is a hope that goes beyond the hope of the past of simply integrating people. . . . The word inclusion acknowledges a history of exclusion that we have to overcome' (Florian et al., 1998:15).

Inclusion is the opposite of exclusion; it acknowledges exclusion and works to counter it.

Commonality of language

The language used to describe inclusion can be interpreted as the essence of inclusion. Definitions of inclusion describe a process or situation in which barriers are removed from participation and students are educated within an environment that is the least restrictive. Yell describes this as: "LRE is a principle stating that students with disabilities are to be educated in settings as close to regular classes as appropriate for the child" (Yell, 1995: 193).

- **Inclusion emphasises the removal of barriers**
- **Inclusion acknowledges people – they are made visible and are valued**
- **Inclusion is about community, people are educated together**

Inclusion within a school setting

Progressive schools have been at the forefront of defining inclusion and inclusive practices. Rouse and Florian describe effective inclusive schools as 'diverse problem-solving organisations with a common mission that emphasises learning for all students' (Skidmore, 2004:22).

This approach to inclusion demonstrates that schools that are effective in inclusive practice are problem solving. This suggests an environment that is not fixed but in flux, one that is problem solving and proactive as opposed to reactive. Through these processes and within these situations students receive a meaningful education as active participants.

- **Inclusion focuses on problem solving**
- **Inclusion emphasises learning for all**
- **Inclusion emphasises active participation**

Having an inclusive approach means that you anticipate and mitigate barriers; you plan for them and have a flexible approach to problem solving them as they present. An inclusive approach also means that you are aware of different opportunities when they arise, that you value these and build on them to inform the process of learning. Inclusion is also non-hierarchical; it acknowledges all that are involved in the process of learning.

- **Inclusion is non-hierarchical**
- **Inclusion anticipates need**

Process over product

Valuing participation

Inclusion is a humanising approach to learning. Inclusion acknowledges the person at every stage, and it focuses on the process of learning. This acknowledges that learning can be different for a range of learners and that the focus is on the process of the learning and not the product or end point.

Inclusion values the process of learning and the learning journey.

Co-production

Co-production describes an approach to the development of a project or programme of projects.

The distinctive feature of co-production is that the design of the project and the decision-making process is inclusive of the participants. Co-production firmly situates the relationship as one of collaboration. The benefits of this approach to project design and development are that it is inclusive of the insights and views of the participants; it increases engagement and the impact of the project. It enables the facilitators and participants to work together as equals and through this it can help to increase confidence of the participants and help them to build skills. This can be seen when schools work with cultural organisations to develop programming. More information and specific examples of co-production can be found in chapters 8 and 10.

Relationships are central to inclusive practice.
Engagement is a central tenet of inclusion.

Language of inclusion

As we can see there are a number of words associated with inclusion. All of these terms will be useful language in guiding you on your journey to increasing inclusion and inclusive practice.

A working definition of inclusion

These descriptions of inclusion are subjective and dependent on interpretation. Can a definition be distilled from these variations? I think so – the subjective nature chimes with the notion of active and meaningful participation. The potency of inclusion is that it is anchored in the subjective; it directly correlates to the individual's experience.

So, I will use the terms to provide a simple working definition of inclusion:

> **Inclusion and inclusive practice happen in the least restrictive environment when all are involved in meaningful and active participation through the removal of barriers.**

How we will use this definition and the language associated in this book

The definition will be the yardstick that we will apply throughout this book to consider and describe inclusion. The associated words will also be used to help in these descriptions.

Practical advice and guidance

Inclusive language

The following table gives examples of what these descriptions might look like.

Inclusive language	How this might present/look/be supported
Inclusion is the mechanism and process by which these groups are included	• Always greet people and acknowledge them, ask what name they would like to be called • Be open to make changes and accommodate • Always give choice and acknowledge it
Inclusion is the opposite of exclusion; it acknowledges exclusion and works to counter it	• Discuss with colleagues and participants when they might have felt excluded and how it could be resolved • The resolution can be both attitudinal and addressing physical issues; on a trip this might be the practical support in accessing the space and the travel arrangements before – consider all these aspects when planning • Some solutions can be 'best fit' and can show how a long-term problem might be solved
Inclusion emphasises the removal of barriers	• Have honest conversations emphasising that all are involved in the process of inclusion and in identifying barriers and possible solutions
Inclusion acknowledges people – they are made visible and are valued	• Acknowledge all people and consider how their voice might be heard; this could be through additional resources for those who find oracy difficult • Find out and anticipate this need • Use projects/processes that make people visible and where difference is seen and celebrated • Stories and personal narratives are powerful tools in this process
Inclusion is about community; people are educated together	• Emphasise community as part of any process • Consider the entry points for a range of learners in projects, signpost them, make them known and valued
Inclusion focuses on problem solving	• If a different/more engaging way of doing something presents, act on it! Part of the process is the learning and new knowledge it presents
Inclusion emphasises learning for all Inclusion emphasises active participation	• Equal value and equally celebrated • Engagement is a central tenet of inclusion • Consider what young people enjoy, what their interests are. This will support deeper learning and can give you the context and space that will allow you to extend and build. • Remember, inclusion considers knowledge – how it is experienced and acted upon in real-world situations
Inclusion is non-hierarchical Inclusion anticipates need	• All are equal, valued, and respected throughout • Consider and anticipate need, find out information, consider and mitigate barriers • Talk and plan together, take advice, adapt, make changes, and build rapport • What practical resources might be needed to support learners and increase engagement? • What are their entry points? Articulate, share, and value these points of entry • What are their ages? • What are their cognition and learning needs? • What are their individual needs? Are there any key pieces of information that would need to be considered? • Timings and structures – some learners may engage for short periods and need to walk between activities. What is the optimum time for an activity? • Access to toilets, snacks etc. Do people know where to go? • Check in, 'is everyone okay?' Ask questions and make changes as the project/visit progresses

Inclusive language	How this might present/look/be supported
Inclusion values the process of learning and the learning journey Relationships are central to inclusive practice Engagement is a central tenet of inclusion	• Describe the learning as a process, celebrate the process – highlight this and give it value, describe what people are doing – give it voice • Build rapport and trust and ask for views and opinions and act on them • Consider what this looks like – learners shouldn't be passive • Engagement varies depending on the learner; find out what they engage in/like – use this knowledge and build on it • Work with the learner to increase engagement. How can you support and increase this engagement? If they are painting, offer different colours or see if they would like to add glitter . . . can they collect their resources, are they signposted, are you promoting choice and independence?

Inclusive evaluations and assessments

'Assessment' comes from the Latin '*assidere*', which means to sit beside.

Assessment and evaluation capture a biographical chapter in both a young person, and or an organisation. When we think of inclusive evaluation it is important to remember this. In the table below gives you some guiding principles of evaluation

Principles of inclusive assessment and evaluation	How this might present/look/be supported
Assessment and evaluation should always emphasise what someone achieved/what someone did/what happened, not what wasn't achieved/what someone didn't do/what didn't happen Meaningful communication	• Assessment should be positive, focusing on what the learner is able to do and needs to do next • Consider wording/language used in capturing information • Find out the best way to communicate/capture information prior to the workshop/project **For more complex students:** • This could be affectations – how the young person responds during the activity; smiles, extended engagement – find out and ask familiar members of staff to comment on this • This could be the level/time they remained engaged **Other ways of collecting information:** • Through symbols – based on the learner's experience, use an understanding of symbols – find out and ask, if it would be appropriate • Capturing information while it's happening – be descriptive and consider what they did and how • Through anecdotal comments captured during their active participation • Through open questions posed at the end/on reflection • Capturing information from the teacher/facilitators, consider what you wanted to achieve, but any other useful comments *** keep it simple, simple language and questions; to make the information collection easier, build it into the workshop/ project design. Information can be made on reflection and on post-it notes – it doesn't have to be arduous** *** remember, keeping it simple and easy to manage will increase the chances of it being sustainable**
Consider multiple tools and methods to ensure that all are included in the process of evaluating	• To create a whole picture, use different tools that are meaningful for all involved. The can be descriptive/anecdotal in nature and/or based on the participant's responses, levels of engagement (time) based on prior knowledge of the learner • They can take the form of a celebratory event • They can also be part of the structure as reflective exercise within the structure of the project/workshop • Consider prior knowledge of the young person; this can be in the form of a written description or what they engage or like in the art/drama/music/dance lesson – keep it brief and simple. It will give you something to relate to/from • Keep it simple! Simple forms/simple language
Holistic assessment	• Case studies are great ways of pulling all this information together in a holistic manner
Descriptive	• Descriptive assessment aligns with inclusion. It tells the story of assessment, how and in what way; it is subjective and biographical and offers insights on how and in what way to develop

Concluding notes

Assessment is a common theme that is explored throughout the book in various situations, and practical guidance is given to support you in your journey towards greater inclusion. More information on case studies and their practical use can be found in chapter 10, and also included is a guide on how to structure case studies. Specific examples of inclusive assessment for describing learning can be found in chapters 8 and 9.

References

Florian, L., Rose, R. and Tilstone, C. (1998) *Promoting Inclusive Practice*. London: Routledge.

Forlin, C. (2010) *Teacher Education for Inclusion: Changing Paradigms and Innovative Approaches*. Oxon: Routledge.

Skidmore, D. (2004) *Inclusion: The Dynamics of School Development*. Maidenhead: Open University.

3 Shaping a culturally inclusive curriculum

Introduction

This chapter focuses on how schools can build a culturally inclusive curriculum for the twenty-first century. It poses the question, how do schools build a **sense of place** through arts and culture? It takes a practical view of how schools can develop it and looks at how culture is located in the curriculum. The chapter does by examining the pre-existing lenses of the SEND code of practice (2015), SMSC (spiritual, moral, social, and cultural) development, and British Values and demonstrates how schools can shape positive identities and more inclusive societies. It also considers what cultural capital is and how it can be understood and defined in schools.

The chapter is designed to support the development of a culturally inclusive curriculum. It takes a practical approach to assisting those who work in both schools and the cultural sector and examines how the curriculum can be built. It also defines some of the most common terminology used; this is to ensure that there is a shared common language so that we are all confident in the terms used and what they refer to across these spaces.

In conversations with cultural organisations, a common theme identified was a gap in knowledge around some of the structures and systems that educational settings use and work within. This chapter will bridge the gap between cultural institutions and educational settings to increase understanding between these two key players.

How to use this chapter

The chapter contains mapping and auditing tools that can support settings in capturing and valuing what they already do and will help in defining the next steps in supporting the development of a culturally inclusive curriculum. The tools will help settings to locate this learning, and the action plan, in their school practices.

The code of practice for SEND, student voice, and co-production; how to build inclusion through practice

The code of practice for SEND: 0–25 years

The SEND code of practice (2015) is the statutory guidance for organisations which work with and support children and young people, from the ages of 0 to 25, who have special educational needs or disabilities.

Choice within the SEND code of practice

Choice is referenced 20 times in the document. The concept of choice is fundamental to the notion of creative and artistic practice. Developing a sense of self and being able to express it, to mediate our experiences of the world, is in part a description of culture and cultural production. The elasticity of the arts and culture allows individuals to both experience and understand the world through exploration and expression.

The code also states that

> 'It can be particularly powerful to meet disabled adults who are a successful in their work, or who have made significant contribution to their community'.
> 'High aspirations about employment, independent living and community participation should be developed through the curriculum and extra-curriculum provision'
>
> (SEN Code of Practice, 2015:124).

Developing a canon that is inclusive and shows the importance of promoting role models is made clear. We will explore this theme briefly in this chapter and in more depth in chapter 6, which covers disability-led organisations.

DOI: 10.4324/9781003122258-3

Contextualising the curriculum

To understand the current curriculum I have framed it within the wider context and the notion of a broad and balanced curriculum that includes the SMSC agenda and cultural capital, which have recently been added to the Ofsted School inspection handbook.

The language of curriculum

What is a curriculum?

The term curriculum refers to the body of knowledge and skills and the content that you wish to transmit to the children or young people that you teach.

Pedagogy

Another important aspect of teaching is to understand the distinction between curriculum and pedagogy. Curriculum refers to the content, and pedagogy refers to the transmission of knowledge through the practice of teaching.

Planning: the anticipation of need

Planning in relation to inclusive practice refers to the anticipation of need to both support and facilitate learning. It is useful to think of this as a framework in which learning can take place.

The act of planning within an inclusive curriculum usually is a joint activity that involves all those who will be supporting the delivery of the curriculum. Through professional conversation, various entry points into the curriculum are mapped so that all learners can access the curriculum in an appropriate and meaningful way. It is important to recognise that **all entry points are of equal value**.

An inclusive approach also acknowledges that learning is opportunity based; when an opportunity to support learning arises, it is acknowledged and built upon. This can be through a learner-led approach, or assessment for learning, more commonly known as AfL.

A continuum of knowledge

An inclusive curriculum recognises that knowledge isn't siloed into distinctive areas; it views knowledge as a continuum that is made up of various subjects. This approach is similar to how knowledge is experienced, shared, and enacted in the world around us.

Delivered through the lens of inclusion

It is also important to note here that within an inclusive curriculum knowledge is delivered through the lens of inclusion. This refers to the way in which the teaching takes place in relation to the individual learners' needs and how best to support their learning. This is often described as person centred, or person centric.

Pupil voice

Pupil voice describes the mechanisms through which learners actively participate in their learning and influence the decisions that inform this participation.

Engagement

Engagement is seen as a central tenet of inclusion; it is here that the most profound learning can take place.

What do we mean by a culturally inclusive curriculum?

A legal requirement

Maintained schools have obligations under **section 78 of the Education Act (2002)** which requires schools, as part of a broad and balanced curriculum, to promote the spiritual, moral, cultural, mental, and physical development of pupils.

Culture is central to curriculum

The requirement recognises the importance of culture and its centrality within the curriculum. It also prescribes that access to a broad and balanced curriculum is a legal obligation. The school has a legal duty to promote culture, and that culture is situated alongside spiritual, social, moral, mental, and physical development of young people. **This is what supports our children and young people in becoming fully included, actualised, and valued members of society**.

The broad view: how is culture located within the curriculum?

We will now explore how culture is situated within the wider school curriculum. This is an initial exercise to map the curriculum in relation to the SMSC agenda as a starting point, the shape of the curriculum, and a direction of travel. This will give you the ability to understand these themes in relation to curriculum in the broadest sense; it is also part of a school's or setting's duty to articulate this. From here, we will then make further enquiry within the areas listed as follows:

- **Local community**
- **Wider/national community**
- **An alternative canon**
- **Cultural capital**

Exercise 1 – mapping your curriculum in relation to the SMSC agenda

One method that is useful for understanding the shape, scope, and content of your curriculum, and being able to articulate it, is to map your curriculum with colleagues as an exercise.

This activity will allow you and your colleagues to understand your curriculum better. The process is designed to support professional dialogue and reflection in order to further deepen understanding of the context in which you work. It will enable you to articulate and signpost it, to celebrate it, and to help you identify where opportunities exist to develop content and how you might do this.

Activity – mapping your curriculum in relation to SMSC

The following is an example of a mapping exercise.

To start this process, it is preferable to organise it within a pre-existing programme of school development and improvement meetings where all members of the school community are present. To increase the impact of the exercise it is good practice to explain the purposes of the meeting and the intended outcomes.

These could be:

1. To familiarise yourself with the SMSC agenda and to map this into your curriculum
2. To discuss the Ofsted descriptors and adapt them to make them pertinent to (insert school name) so that they can inform the development of a culturally inclusive curriculum.

When locating these descriptors in your environment/setting, it is important to remember:

- Some of these descriptors may not apply in their totality – that's okay
- They can be adapted and interpreted within your local setting

★ *To demonstrate and understand this fully is good practice. To examine all aspects of your curriculum and to gain better understanding of SMSC will provide your school with meaningful evidence for Ofsted to demonstrate your school's understanding of this central aspect of your curriculum.*

Next steps

With a mapped curriculum area, you will then know areas of development.

Before undertaking your mapping exercise, familiarise yourself with the SMSC descriptors

Social

- Use of a range of social skills in different contexts, including working and socialising with pupils from different religious, ethnic, and socioeconomic backgrounds
- Willingness to participate in a variety of social settings, cooperating well with others, and being able to resolve conflicts effectively with an interest in, and understanding of, the way communities and societies function at a variety of levels

---

Moral

- Ability to recognise the difference between right and wrong and a readiness to apply this understanding in their own lives
- Understanding of the consequences of their actions and interest in investigating and offering reasoned views about moral and ethical issues

Spiritual

- Beliefs, religious or otherwise, which inform their perspective on life and their interest in and respect for different people's feelings and values
- Sense of enjoyment and fascination in learning about themselves, others, and the world around them. Including the intangible use of imagination and creativity in their learning and a willingness to reflect on their experiences

Cultural

- Understanding and appreciation of the wide range of cultural influences that have shaped their own heritage. A willingness to participate in, and respond to, for example, artistic, musical, sporting, mathematical, technological, scientific, and cultural opportunities
- Interest in exploring, an understanding of, and a respect for cultural diversity and the extent to which they understand, accept, respect, and celebrate diversity. Shown by their attitudes towards different religious, ethnic, and socioeconomic groups in local, national, and global communities

Below shows how this activity can be undertaken

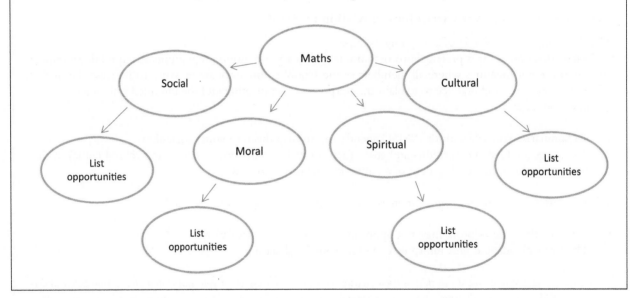

The local and national community

Place-based identities

Another characteristic of an inclusive school is that they are outward facing and community oriented.

Local identities and local cultures

This will be explored in relation to the work of the Royal Society of Arts (RSA) in this area. In their August 2020 report, Heritage for Inclusive Growth, they describe these strategies as:

> 'Utilising and supporting the heritage assets and activities within a place to create sustainable, equitably distributed growth and to enable the development of inclusive place-based identities'
>
> (RSA, Heritage for inclusive growth, 2020:11)

Here we have the beginnings of what constitutes the notion of a local cultural offer. The RSA goes on further to pose the question:

> 'What makes a community feel like home? How does local history shape local identity? Can a sense of belonging make a place better to live in?'
>
> (Taken from the RSA website)

Why is this important?

It is crucial to increasing community cohesion and ensuring a place for all. A fundamental part of the process is developing more inclusive language to describe your offer and more accessible ways of communicating it. As the RSA states in Heritage for Inclusive Growth (2020):

> 'Key to this is establishing a more inclusive narrative about the value that a sense of place, community and belonging has for everyone and the importance of centring space for a plurality of heritages and voices within this'
>
> (RSA, Heritage for Inclusive growth, 2020:13)

Schools and cultural organisations are central in local identities

Although this example refers to the heritage sector, it can be applied to other places of culture and demonstrates the importance of being seen, acknowledged, and valued within your community. It also relates directly to the notion of social role valorisation (SRV) as discussed in the Introduction.

Exercise 2 – mapping your local area and describing your place-based identity

Activity: mapping your local area and writing a statement that describes your place-based identity

We know that inclusion is increased when relationships are built and developed over time.

You need to invest time to build rapport and understand each other so that you can work to maximum effect. The following table will help you consider the location of your setting and your relationships within this area. This will enable you to articulate your **place-based identity and how it promotes inclusion**.

Consider these three principles when undertaking this exercise

- Consider your local character, geography, history, and location and write a statement to articulate it. For example: *We are a central London multicultural school; we have established partnerships that reflect the diversity of our population and make good use of our local cultural assets*
- Consider how and why you are engaging with partners. It is useful for increasing understanding and therefore impact
- Practice: who are they? What do they offer? What do you offer them? Consider the opportunities for co-production

★ The statement could relate to your school's mission statement, as it is always good to make this pertinent to your community.

Within the school	Within the local community	Description: who/what are they? What is the practice?	Impact: how does it promote inclusion?
Rationale: The table is designed to capture information that describes the cultural offer within the school community and within the local community and asks, how does this promote inclusion?			
International evening			Students have the opportunity to share their cultural heritage and bring their family history into school. Home/family/school relationships acknowledged

The wider national context

The national picture gives you a view beyond the local community and demonstrates how the school is mediating and including the school community within the wider national discourse.

The following activity captures the school's access to, and participation in, the wider national cultural life of the country. It also demonstrates how this translates into an educational setting and explores how it can be supported and extended to promote inclusion.

Exercise 3 – mapping cultural engagement nationally

Activity: mapping the school's engagement with culture within the wider national context

The following table is similar to the earlier table in which you mapped local opportunities. This table looks at the wider national context.

Consider

- Consider how and why you are engaging with partners. It is useful to increase understanding and therefore impact.
- Consider practice: who are partners, what do you offer them?

Wider national context	Description: who/what are they? What is the practice/ initiative?	Impact: how does it promote inclusion?
Rationale: The table is designed to capture information that describes how the school engages within the wider national context		

Cultural capital and cultural inclusion

Cultural capital and the education debate: how it came about

Cultural capital has recently been included in the Ofsted Schools inspection handbook. The inclusion of this model has gained attention within the general education debate, and more specifically around the notion of social mobility.

The movement towards both valuing and evidencing culture in a more formalised manner can be traced back to the inception of the new national curriculum under the auspices of the then Sectary of State for Education Michael Gove in 2014. Although the framework that was published did not directly use the term *cultural capital*, the language that the Ofsted guidance uses makes direct reference to the terminology used within the national curriculum. It describes this knowledge as essential:

> 'The national curriculum provides pupils with an introduction to the essential knowledge they need to be educated citizens. It introduces pupils to the best that has been thought and said, and helps engender an appreciation of human creativity and achievement'.
>
> (National Curriculum in England, 2014:6)

Cultural capital: what is it, and what are its implications for inclusion?

Cultural capital refers to the skills, knowledge, and attitudes that are associated with the dominant class, in other words, the dominant middle class. It encapsulates education, style, accent, speech, and also physical appearance.

Cultural capital is constructed through the cultural experiences and discourses that young people are exposed to in the home via their parents. An example is reading, but with emphasis on those texts that can be described as classic or have a perceived higher cultural value. Visiting galleries and museums and holidaying abroad to 'broaden their horizons' are further examples of practices that imbue those young people with value: cultural capital.

The cultural practices and knowledge that are passed on to children from their parents and caregivers are described as cultural reproduction. Their value is not monetary or financial capital. Cultural capital directly correlates with the ability to progress in society; this is described as social mobility.

Terminology in relation to cultural capital

Embodied state

The form of knowledge that resides within us.

Objectified state

Material objects that indicate social status such as cars and trainers.

Institutionalised state

The way that society measures social capital. This is where both tensions and opportunities arise and will be explored within this chapter.

Pierre Bourdieu, the inventor of cultural capital

> *The cultural knowledge that serves as currency that helps us navigate culture and alters our experiences and the opportunities available to us.*
>
> Pierre Bourdieu (2015)

Pierre Bourdieu

Pierre Bourdieu (01 August 1930–23 January 2002) was a French sociologist, anthropologist, philosopher, and public intellectual. He was a major contributor to the sociology of education. Bourdieu's influence can be found within the field of education and aesthetics, popular culture and the arts. One of the most influential sociological concepts that he developed was that of cultural capital. The argument that this model furthered for Bourdieu was the notion that capital was entrenched within one section of society.

Cultural capital and schools

Bourdieu, who developed the concept of cultural capital, mainly considered this within a family structure with school playing an acknowledged role within the transmission of cultural capital and also as one of the signifiers of value.

Cultural capital and Ofsted

'Inspectors will consider the extent to which schools are equipping pupils with the knowledge and cultural capital they need to succeed in life (Ofsted, School inspection handbook, 2022:48) Our understanding of "knowledge and cultural capital" is derived from the following wording in the national curriculum: "The national curriculum provides pupils with an introduction to the essential knowledge that they need to be educated citizens. It introduces pupils to the best that has been thought and said; and helps engender an appreciation of human creativity and achievement"

(National Curriculum in England, 2014: 6)

All educational settings in the UK will now be judged on how they support, deliver, and provide students with cultural capital. This chimes with Ofsted's move away from purely quantitative measures of progress and towards the use and promotion of qualitative measures of progress with a particular emphasis in relation to SEND.

Implications for Ofsted ratings

The implications for schools and early years settings is that they cannot receive a rating of 'good' unless their curriculum gives '*all pupils, particularly disadvantaged pupils . . . the knowledge and cultural capital they need to succeed in life*' (Ofsted, School inspection handbook, 2022:45). This will obviously increase schools' awareness of cultural capital as well as how to articulate it, measure it, and develop it for their students.

Tensions within Ofsted interpretation

The introduction of cultural capital into the Ofsted framework does herald a move to a more inclusive approach to judgments and signals an appreciation of a richer curriculum offer and more inclusive model of education. However, there are tensions surrounding the use of this term and its associated discourse that give cause for concern.

Institutionalised state: one type of culture?

Bourdieu originally used the model to challenge the notion of **one type of culture as dominant** and superior to that of others. The concern here is that there is a preconceived notion of what constitutes culture. This creates the threat of imposing one view of what is considered to be culture on a society and, as a result, denying the value of the less dominant culture. This has wide implications. Helen Moylett, Early Years Consultant and writer, wrote:

Such cavalier use of this term is likely to perpetuate deficit models of working-class children (and many other children who are not white, British and middle class).

(Moylett 2019)

So, what of cultural inclusion within this model? There is a danger here that needs to be challenged, as there is the possibility of exclusion

When all children should access this, how do we articulate and quantify what is 'the best that has been thought and said'?

Integration versus inclusion

The issue here is that the there is an assumption that only one type of knowledge/culture has value, one that could be presumed to be conservative in nature, white and middle class. This then presents the notion of **integration** and not of **inclusion**.

Here you can see the importance of cultural inclusion. Both the model of cultural capital and social role valorisation emphasise the value of imagery and ideas that can support society's view/value of someone and the impact that this has on their quality of life.

If we are to be more progressive within this space and become more inclusive in both education and society, we need to acknowledge that education can only go so far. If we are to be truly effective, all of society needs to be included within the debate.

An opportunity: cultural capital and inclusion, celebrating difference and visibility

The opportunity here is that we all have the ability in the various spaces and settings that we work in to promote an inclusive culture.

We can use this theory to our advantage by articulating, developing, and promoting a model of cultural capital that is inclusive. One which makes our young people visible as both producers and consumers of culture. A model that corresponds with social role valorisation and through this construct increases their capital and value and ultimately their life chances.

Exercise 4 – articulating and building cultural capital

How can schools build cultural capital?

We have demonstrated in the activities within this chapter how your school is supporting strategic access to arts and culture. These activities also demonstrate the access to culture and cultural capital.

Supporting cultural capital in everyday teaching

This happens through everyday practice in activities such as:

- Playing with games and toys
- Books and stories
- Songs
- Class and whole-school celebrations

Cultural capital in the early years

Within the early years cultural capital is framed within those activities that support child development. The language that frames cultural capital within the framework uses the terminology of supporting young people's experience in the '**awe and wonder**' of the world. This means children experiencing and participating in high-quality arts activities. It's the cultural knowledge that supports play and development. Play takes place in a cultural context through **fun** and **engaging activities**.

At this stage of education children arrive at these settings having a wide range of different experiences in their learning and play. It is through the settings' interactions and facilitations that they collectively experience structured play through the early years foundation stage curriculum and the seven areas of learning:

- communication and language
- physical development
- personal, social, and emotional development
- literacy
- mathematics
- understanding the world
- expressive arts and design

Cultural capital is securely embedded across all these areas, as the main vehicle of learning is play, and part of your everyday delivery could include activities such as:

- Finding books on a child's favourite topic that engage them and promote their interest
- Developing and extending this further by creating role-play activities that further their interest in a particular idea
- Community walks and taking trips to the park to play
- Organising visits from community figures such as members of the fire service, police, and so on

Mapping exercise

As with the SMSC mapped earlier in the chapter as an activity, there is lots of commonality with cultural capital in how you can both evidence and articulate it. Understanding that cultural capital is present in everyday practice can be useful for empowering teachers and supporting their understanding of this terminology.

Developing a statement that defines cultural capital within your school's specific context

The previous mapping exercises will have generated content to help you develop your statement in articulating aspects of cultural capital successfully.

To be able to describe how your children and young people access those cultural activities that are generated within the school community and the wider context, it is important to remember that they themselves are producers of art and culture. Considering this alongside some of the statements as detailed later will ensure that you are creating a dynamic statement where you place inclusion and cultural capital within the same framework.

Activity: workshop on anchoring the descriptor in the school's practices

Developing a statement where you define what is

'The essential knowledge that pupils need to be educated citizens, introducing them to the best that has been thought and said and helping to engender an appreciation of human creativity and achievement' as described by Ofsted Education Inspection Framework.

(Ofsted, Schools inspection handbook, 2022:48)

Consider the statement and your cultural offer at both the local and the national level and how this supports the statement within the SEND code of practice (2015) as mentioned previously:

'It can be particularly powerful to meet disabled adults who are a successful in their work, or who have made significant contribution to their community'

(SEN Code of Practice, 2015:124)

This is the space where inclusion and cultural capital meet within the location of an inclusive school. Use both of these descriptors within your statement to demonstrate that the access that the school provides to increase cultural capital also increases the value of the students themselves; it reflects them and values them.

Concluding notes

One important point here is the notion of the role model, the canon of those artists who are reflective of the neurodivergent, D/deaf, and disabled community and allow children and young people to see themselves within those spaces and place. This is a theme that will be examined further in chapter 6.

References

Moylett, H. (2019). "Ofsted's thinking on Cultural Capital". *Early Education*. [online]. Available at: https://www.early-education.org. uk/news/guest-blog-helen-moylett-ofsted%E2%80%99s-thinking-cultural-capital-some-concerns-and-questions [Accessed on 29 Oct 2019].

Sociology Live. (2015). "Cultural Capital". *YouTube*, uploaded Nov 17, 2015, www.youtube.com/watch?v=5DBEYiBkgp8

Special educational needs and disability code of practice: 0 to 25 years Statutory guidance for organisations which work with and support children and young people who have special educational needs or disabilities January 2015

The National Curriculum in England, Framework document, 2014 Ofsted, School inspection handbook, 2022

4 Policy and strategy – implications for cultural inclusion – know your rights!

This chapter will tell you how to exercise your rights and where to seek advice. Schools as public bodies also need to comply with the legal requirement and to demonstrate how they are meeting these obligations.

A question of morality

The arguments for inclusion are historical and well documented. Central to these arguments are the notions of equality and human rights. There is a moral imperative to these arguments, that inclusion respects every individual and values them. It sees difference and diversity as a rich resource that enriches all of society.

Understanding the policy landscape and your rights and obligations

It is crucial to examine cultural inclusion within the context of the developing international, national, and local policy landscape. International treaties, including the UN Convention on the Rights of Disabled People 2006 and the EU Framework designed to implement it, have had an enormous impact on disabled people's rights in signatory countries across the world. At the national level, the UK Disability Discrimination Acts (1995, 2005, and 2010) have made an invaluable contribution to the daily lives of people with disabilities by conferring specific rights on them across a range of sectors.

How to use this chapter

This chapter's intention is to give you a clear understanding of the legal frameworks and how they describe these rights. Rights that determine how and in what way people have legal access to participate in society.

These legal frameworks have a huge impact on all aspects of people's lives, and they inform how both educational spaces and cultural settings institutions operate and organise themselves.

Embedding rights within the curriculum

This chapter also looks at how these rights are expressed within present education policy, and it looks at how these can be supported and taught within school's settings using the Rights Respecting Schools programme so that students and whole school communities can become advocates and active citizens.

How inclusion is enacted through a legal framework

If you work in the space of arts, culture, and inclusion, legal frameworks will directly shape the work that you do, how you do it, and the legal obligations that inform your work. To understand this framework will enhance your understanding and increase your impact.

Inclusion and the rights of disabled people have been embedded within a number of national and international legal frameworks. These frameworks have a direct impact on the lives of disabled people and how **inclusion is enacted**.

It is important to have some understanding of these frameworks, as this will give you a deeper understanding of the space.

A framework that informs your work

This chapter lays out the **key dates** of the **legal frameworks** that support both disability rights and inclusion. This chapter will cover four pieces of key pieces of legislation:

* The Equality Act 2010
* The UN Convention on the Rights of Persons with Disabilities (2006, ratified in the UK 2009)

DOI: 10.4324/9781003122258-4

- Salamanca Statement, 1994 (adopted by the World Conference on Special Needs Education: Access and Quality (Salamanca, Spain, 7–10 June 1994)
- The United Nations Rights of the Child 1990

How can an individual or an organisation enforce legislation?

The chapter is also designed to make you aware of your rights and obligations and to signpost how you can enforce these so that you can confidently self-advocate.

Themes of legislation

This chapter will summarise the intention of the legislation. It categorises the legislation into different headings that cover the following themes and their applicability to education:

- **Discrimination**
- **Access and equality**
- **Inclusion**
- **Human rights**

Resources and practical printouts

The information that references the legislation and the articles that directly reference disability are on single sheets for easier copying and display purposes.

Date and title: The Equality Act 2010

Theme: discrimination

The Equality Act 2010 says that you must not be discriminated against because:

- You have a disability
- Someone thinks you have a disability (this is known as discrimination by perception)
- You are connected to someone with a disability (this is known as discrimination by association)
- It is not unlawful discrimination to treat a disabled person more favourably than a nondisabled person

The Equality Act 2010 describes discrimination in relation to disability as:
   Discrimination arising from disability occurs when a disabled pupil is treated unfavourably because something related to his/her disability (as distinct from being because of the disability itself, which would be **direct discrimination**) and such treatment cannot be justified. The following conditions must be met:

- The disabled pupil is treated in a way which puts him/her at disadvantage
- The treatment is connected with the pupil's disability
- The treatment cannot be justified as 'proportionate means of achieving a legitimate aim'

Failure to make reasonable adjustments for disabled people. There has been a duty on responsible bodies of schools to make reasonable adjustments for disabled pupils and prospective pupils since 1995. The new act extends the duty so that a school must also provide auxiliary aids and services.
   * The responsible body for schools is the Department for Education (DFE) and those bodies that sit within the DFE.
   The act states that the responsible body of a school must not discriminate against a person in its:

- Admissions arrangements
- Provision of education
- Exclusions or by subjecting the pupil to any other detriment

Date and title: The UN Convention on the Rights of Persons with Disabilities (2006, ratified in the UK in 2009)

Theme: inclusion, access and equality, and discrimination

Article 5 recognises the right to equality and nondiscrimination; article 7 makes special provision for children; article 24 asserts the right to inclusive education.

Signatories to the Convention recognise:

> the importance of accessibility to the physical, social, economic and cultural environment, to health and education and to information and communication, in enabling persons with disabilities to fully enjoy all human rights and fundamental freedoms.

> (Preamble, para. v)

Below are some extracts of the Convention

(1) States Parties recognize the right of persons with disabilities to education. With a view to realizing this right without discrimination and on the basis of equal opportunity, States Parties shall ensure an inclusive education system at all levels and lifelong learning directed to:

   a.   the development by persons with disabilities of their personality, talents and creativity, as well as their mental and physical abilities, to their fullest potential;
   b.   enabling persons with disabilities to participate effectively in a free society.

Date and title: Salamanca Statement, 1994 (Adopted by the World Conference on Special Needs Education: Access and Quality (Salamanca, Spain, 7–10 June 1994)

Theme: inclusion

> The statement calls on the international community to endorse the approach of inclusive schools by implementing practical and strategic changes.

Education for all

> The statement makes a commitment to education for all. The statement makes a commitment to education for all and states that that this should take place within the **regular education system**. It states, 'young people must have access to regular schools'
> It goes on to state:

> Regular schools with this inclusive orientation are the most effective means of combating discriminatory attitudes, **creating welcoming communities**, **building an inclusive society**, and achieving education for all; moreover, they provide an effective education to the majority of children and improve the efficiency and ultimately the cost-effectiveness of the entire education system.

And:

> Inclusion and participation are essential to human dignity and to the enjoyment and exercise of human rights.

Date and Title: The United Nations Rights of the Child 1990

Theme: human rights

The most widely ratified human rights instrument is the UN Rights of the Child, to which the UK is also a signatory. The United Nations Rights of the Child has a **treaty monitoring body**. The body monitors its implementation in all signatory state parties.

The United Nations Rights of the Child is a comprehensive framework and upholds children's rights all over the world. It contains **54 articles** that cover all aspects of a **child's** life and sets out the civil, political, economic, social, and cultural rights that all **children** everywhere are entitled to and is the basis for all of UNICEF's work

The United Nations Rights of the Child is the most widely ratified international human rights treaty in history.

The two articles that directly reference both disability and arts and culture are:

23. Children with disabilities

Every child with a disability should enjoy the best possible life in society. Governments should remove all obstacles for children with disabilities to become independent and to participate actively in the community.

31. Rest, play, culture, arts

Every child has the right to rest, relax, play, and to take part in cultural and creative activities.

The Equality and Human Rights Commission

The Equality and Human Rights Commission is the 'national equality body' for the whole of the United Kingdom. It is legally required by statute to promote:

Understanding of the importance of and encourage good practice in relation to equality and diversity; promote equality of opportunity; promote awareness and understanding of rights under the Equality Act; enforce the Equality Act; and work towards the elimination of unlawful discrimination and unlawful harassment.

(Taken from House of Commons Women and Equalities Committee Enforcing the Equality Act: the law and the role of the Equality and Human Rights Commission Tenth Report of Session 2017–19 Report)

The formation of the Equality and Human Rights Commission

The commission was formed in October 2007 when the commissions on gender, race, and disability merged. It additionally has the responsibilities on religion or belief, sexual orientation, age, gender reassignment, and human rights. It has a wide range of functions, and these include:

* Providing information and advice
* Issuing codes of practice and other guidance
* Advising government on the effects of laws and proposed laws on equality and human rights

The commission also has significant powers to enforce the Equality Act, some of which were inherited from the previous equality commissions.

The Equality Commission's powers

The Equality Act of 2006 gives the commission powers to carry out investigations into compliance with the Equality Act 2010. It also has the powers to:

Investigate

An investigation can be carried out when a person is found to have committed an unlawful act. The commission can also issue notice that an action plan is required.

Action plan

An action plan is a preventative mechanism designed to prevent the unlawful act from happening again.

Assessment of compliance

The commission can assess compliance with the public sector equality duty. The public sector equality duty was initiated as a means of effectively promoting positive equality, shifting the obligation away from the individual, and moving away from just avoiding discrimination.

Public sector equality duty and schools

Schools have a legal duty to comply with the equality duty and show how they have considered the duty in relation to decision making and actions based on their location and needs and in relation to students and staff who have protected characteristics.

Compliance notice

Where a breach of the duty is found, the commission can then issue a compliance notice. It can also require the public authority to supply a written proposal on steps to ensure compliance.

Binding agreements

These agreements can be entered into with organisations when they have committed to or refrained from taking specific actions. This can also be used as an alternative to formal enforcement action.

Injunctions

The commission can apply to the court for an injunction restraining a person from committing an unlawful act.

Unlimited fines enforced by the court

An unlimited fine can also be issued and enforced in court if a breach of notice or a court order is issued under the aforementioned powers.

Support individual complainants to bring a case

This support can also be financial. Additionally, the commission can bring judicial review proceedings in its own name to challenge the decision of a public authority, intervene in cases brought by others, and conduct inquiries that can lead it to making recommendations with potentially wide application.

Be a source of information, advice, and guidance

The commission functions as a provider of education and training and undertakes research. The commission can also issue codes of practice (subject to the approval of the secretary of state).

Tensions within the system

Individuals can enforce the legislation, but this can be problematic. Within this approach the law addresses individual needs, and this is often problematic as it doesn't address systemic issues of discrimination. This can mean that systemic inclusion is hard to achieve and that the structural issue of inclusion isn't addressed.

Contacting the Equality and Human Rights Commission

If you have any questions or concerns in relation to inclusion or discrimination, you can contact them in a number of ways. Their website contains a lot of relevant information and can be accessed at www.equalityhumanrights.com.

The national curriculum, British Values, disability and human rights

The national curriculum requires schools to overtly teach British Values with specific reference to 'mutual respect and understanding' and 'an understanding of the importance of identifying and combatting discrimination' (Promoting fundamental British values as part of SMSC in schools Departmental advice for maintained schools, 2014: pages 5 and 6). They are located within the cultural and spiritual context but do not refer directly to disability awareness. There is an opportunity here, however, as the language chimes with that of the Equality Act 2010 and the United Nations Rights of the Child, which does make direct reference to disabilities:

United Nations Rights of the Child

Article 23. Children with disabilities

> Every child with a disability should enjoy the best possible life in society. Governments should remove all obstacles for children with disabilities to become independent and to participate actively in the community.

These are further supported by articles within the Convention on the Rights of Persons with Disabilities mentioned earlier in the chapter:

Article 7. Children with disabilities

1. States Parties shall take all necessary measures to ensure the full enjoyment by children with disabilities of all human rights and fundamental freedoms on an equal basis with other children.
2. In all actions concerning children with disabilities, the best interests of the child shall be a primary consideration.
3. States Parties shall ensure that children with disabilities have the right to express their views freely on all matters affecting them, their views being given due weight in accordance with their age and maturity, on an equal basis with other children, and to be provided with disability and age-appropriate assistance to realize that right.

Article 8. Awareness-raising

1. States Parties undertake to adopt immediate, effective and appropriate measures:

   a) To raise awareness throughout society, including at the family level, regarding persons with disabilities, and to foster respect for the rights and dignity of persons with disabilities;
   b) To combat stereotypes, prejudices and harmful practices relating to persons with disabilities, including those based on sex and age, in all areas of life;
   c) To promote awareness of the capabilities and contributions of persons with disabilities.

2. Measures to this end include:

   a) Initiating and maintaining effective public awareness campaigns designed:

      i. To nurture receptiveness to the rights of persons with disabilities;
      ii. To promote positive perceptions and greater social awareness towards persons with disabilities;
      iii. To promote recognition of the skills, merits and abilities of persons with disabilities, and of their contributions to the workplace and the labour market.

   b) Fostering at all levels of the education system, including in all children from an early age, an attitude of respect for the rights of persons with disabilities;
   c) Encouraging all organs of the media to portray persons with disabilities in a manner consistent with the purpose of the present Convention;
   d) Promoting awareness-training programmes regarding persons with disabilities and the rights of persons with disabilities.

United Nations Rights of the Child and Rights Respecting Schools

The Convention has 54 articles in total. Articles 43–54 cover how adults and governments must work together to make sure all children can enjoy all their rights.

Cultural organisations have their role to play within this framework too and explicit reference is made to arts and culture:

Children have the right to access artistic activities and culture

Article 31 (leisure, play, and culture) states, 'Every child has the right to relax, play and take part in a wide range of cultural and artistic activities'.

Frame your work in relation to the rights of the child

It is important that cultural spaces realise that children's access is enshrined in law, that they are not only places of education but play and leisure and that the work that they do is valued and is a human right.

It also empowers organisations if they frame the work that they carry out with reference to law. The Rights of the Child are very empowering, and it is hard to refuse or not value the work when it is framed within this context! It is useful to describe it in relation to rights and the message becomes explicit.

Rights Respecting Schools

Schools can be spaces where students' rights are promoted and embedded within the curriculum and the whole school experience. One way that these rights can become central to a student's lived experience is through the use of the **Rights Respecting Schools programme**. This programme embeds the United Nations Rights of the Child within the culture of the school. The programme is a whole school programme that supports children in developing an understanding of their rights and their ability to exercise them.

The award is tiered and demonstrates how the school can increase its awareness and impact of being a Rights Respecting School and embed this within both the school's culture and the curriculum to wide ranging effect. Many schools have used this across the space, from informing school development plans to ensuring that every lesson makes overt links to children's rights. Ultimately, this process has allowed staff and students alike to understand their rights within the framework of education, as well as to self-advocate to realise these rights and to be fully acknowledged and included young people.

Progression through the award helps young people to

- Know about their rights
- Exercise their rights
- Feel valued and empowered
- Understand and recognise the rights of others

Knowledge of these rights helps children recognise what they are entitled to and to challenge when the rights aren't met.

The Rights Respecting Schools Award's evidence of impact and theory of change (the social change that the programme supports) confirms their effectiveness across a number of areas, including:

- Children learn about rights
- Children can exercise their rights
- A culture of respect across the school
- Pupil engagement – a shared sense of community and belonging
- A culture where children's voices are heard and valued
- Children take their right to an education seriously
- Global citizenship – children believe they can change the world for the better
- Children develop self-esteem and value themselves
- A school environment where children feel safe and cared for
- Adults also benefit from a rights respecting culture
- Knowledge and understanding of rights is central to change in these areas since rights not only set standards that children can expect, but also empower children to challenge when these standards are not met.

(Taken from the Rights Respecting Schools website.)

The Rights Respecting Schools and the Equality and Human Rights Commission

The Rights Respecting Schools initiative is acknowledged as good practice in human rights education by the commission. In 2020 it worked with ten schools and presented examples of good practice. It was found that the Rights Respecting Schools Award can support outcomes in many areas of the school but also can have an impact on reducing prejudiced attitudes.

Become a Rights Respecting School

Link the programme overtly to the equality duty that all organisations have in developing a culture that positively supports groups with Rights Respecting Schools: www.unicef.org.uk/rights-respecting-schools

The equality duty and schools

The equality duty has three elements. Public bodies such as schools are required by law to have due regard when developing policies and making decisions to these three elements:

1. Eliminate discrimination, harassment, victimisation, and other conduct that is prohibited by the Equality Act 2010.
2. Advance equality of opportunity between people who share a protected characteristic and people who do not share it.
3. Foster good relations across all protected characteristics – between people who share a protected characteristic and people who do not share it.

These objectives need to be published annually. Schools in England are required to carry out two specific duties to ensure that they are meeting the general equality duty.

These are:

- To publish information to demonstrate how they are complying with the equality duty.
- To prepare and publish one or more specific and measurable equality objective.

  ★ These targets need to be updated annually.

Ofsted and the equality duty

This work will also support schools in showing evidence during Ofsted inspections. The Education Inspection Framework (and Inspection Handbook) outlines the following components that an Ofsted will consider during an inspection:

- As part of their overall evaluation of the school, inspectors will consider the extent to which the education provided by the school meets the needs of the range of pupils at the school, and in particular the needs of disabled pupils and those who have special educational needs
- When evaluating the achievement of pupils, inspectors must consider how well disabled pupils and those who have special educational needs have achieved since joining the school

Supporting effective partnerships

The guidance published by the Equality and Human Rights Commission in relation to the equality duty also outlines:

The equality duty supports effective partnerships by encouraging initiatives among local authorities, schools, parents, carers, and members of local communities. This includes discussions on what actions are needed to improve education for groups of pupils and to foster good relations across all protected characteristics.

Action planning in relation to the equality duty

The following three tables generally support the promotion of the rights explored within this chapter and how and in what way institutions and schools can reinforce these rights in an overt and strategic manner. The ideas can also support schools in their legal obligation to demonstrate that they are addressing objectives developed that comply with the equality duty. A point to note is that the table refers to initiatives that correspond to the elements of the equality duty; however, there is a level of crossover between the three elements and the table refers to just one.

Visibility	*Relationship to equality duty*
Create displays making direct reference to the Rights of the Child and the Equality Act, detailing how and in what way they are lived experience in the school	Advance equality of opportunity between people who share a protected characteristic and people who do not share it
Promote artists that describe themselves as D/deaf, disabled, and neurodivergent, considering the notion of the *inclusive canon* (see chapter 6 titled 'Producers of art and culture: disabled-focused and disabled-led organisations'). This can be in displays, promoted in schemes of work etc.	Foster good relations across all protected characteristics – between people who share a protected characteristic and people who do not share it
Develop an SMSC calendar that raises awareness of disability and ableism. Promote awareness days and links to disabled-led and disability-focused organisations	Advance equality of opportunity between people who share a protected characteristic and people who do not share it
Explore issues-based art, drama, and dance that creates space for discussion and challenges stereotypes and prejudice (see chapter 7 titled 'Cultural inclusion – a historical perspective')	Eliminate discrimination, harassment, victimisation, and other conduct prohibited by the Equality Act 2010
Community	*Relationship to equality duty*
Develop an inclusive arts festival (see chapter 10 titled 'Cultural inclusion; developing meaningful partnerships between schools and cultural organisations. The West London Inclusive Arts Festival') and invite partners and supporters from the local community	Advance equality of opportunity between people who share a protected characteristic and people who do not share it
Develop links to cultural partners that support employment opportunities and role models (see chapter 6 titled 'Producers of art and culture: disabled-focused and disabled-led organisations', which also explores the *Gatsby benchmarks*)	Advance equality of opportunity between people who share a protected characteristic and people who do not share it.

Actively promote inclusion and inclusive practices with partner organisations by adopting a co-production approach to working with outside organisations

Curriculum
Become a Rights Respecting School
Use the inclusive canon and embed people with a diagnosis of hearing impairment, disability, or neurodivergence within schemes of work
Actively challenge stereotypes and ableism overtly. Workshop and challenge these through teacher-led discussions (see chapter 7 titled 'Cultural inclusion – a historical perspective')

Advance equality of opportunity between people who share a protected characteristic and people who do not share it

Impact
All elements
Foster good relations across all protected characteristics – between people who share a protected characteristic and people who do not share it
Eliminate discrimination, harassment, victimisation, and other conduct that is prohibited by the Equality Act 2010.

Concluding notes

This chapter illustrates the importance of being seen and creating environments where all learners can thrive. This chapter outlines how this can be supported. Further practical guidance on anti-ableist pedagogy can be found in chapter 8.

References

Promoting fundamental British values as part of SMSC in schools Departmental advice for maintained schools, 2014.

Further reading and useful contact information

This publication and related equality and human rights resources are available from the Equality and Human Rights Commission's website: www.equalityhumanrights.com.

For advice, information, or guidance on equality, discrimination, or human rights issues, please contact the **Equality Advisory and Support Service**, a free and independent service.

Website: www.equalityadvisoryservice.com
Telephone: 0808 800 0082
Textphone: 0808 800 0084
Hours: 09:00 to 20:00 (Monday to Friday)
10:00 to 14:00 (Saturday)
Post FREEPOST Equality Advisory Support Service FPN4431
Questions and comments regarding this publication may be addressed to correspondence@equalityhumanrights. com. The Commission welcomes your feedback.
Public Sector Equality Duty Guidance for Schools in England published by the Equality and Human Rights Commission
Rights Respecting Schools
Email: rrsa@unicef.org.uk
Phone: 0207 375 6059 (Monday–Friday, 9am–5pm)

5   Cultural inclusion – a family's perspective

The families of disabled children and young people are absolutely central to inclusion. Their lived experiences, and the perspective they gain as a result, are critical to fully understanding the barriers to greater engagement and developing workable solutions to tackle them.

This chapter takes the form of a series of interviews with the parents of disabled children who are active in this space. It profiles four parent activists and looks at their work to promote inclusion in arts and culture in a range of settings and collates their unique views on **representation**, **participation**, and **access**.

How to use this chapter

The focus of the chapter is to harness the expertise of parents of disabled children and young people to identify practical solutions to increase inclusion. Hearing their lived experiences, and understanding their perspective, gives invaluable insight into what does and doesn't work.

In relation to representation, the chapter considers how and in what way authentic storytelling can increase inclusion. It also explores approaches to access and participation and poses questions around what constitutes meaningful access and what this looks like in practice.

The implications of this chapter are focused on two key areas as outlined next.

Educational Implications

The educational implications of this chapter are discussed at the end with practical ideas on how you can work with families in your own local setting. It describes ways that you can include families using arts and culture and how you can build on these interactions to develop positive relationships that are central to a child's success. Schools are often bridges and gateways to the local cultural offer and there is much they can do to support inclusion and enable engagement through effective brokerage.

Cultural sector implications

The interviews are specifically designed to be read by those who work in the cultural sector. Interviewees offer a range ideas, opinions, and guidance that can inform practice. Within the interviews they are asked directly for recommendations, and their responses give those who work in the sector much to consider in terms of their journey to greater inclusion. This is distilled into practical guidance and can be found at the end of the chapter.

How this chapter was written

All interviewees were asked the set of questions outlined next to help guide the conversation and elicit relevant insights.

The questions

Visibility and representation

- What are your views on representation; do you feel there are any examples where disability has been portrayed in a way that is relatable?
- What do you think are characteristics of inclusive authentic portrayal?
- Can you describe why it is important to be authentically portrayed?

DOI: 10.4324/9781003122258-5

Access

I have broken access into six headings. These headings are website accessibility and communication, physical access considerations, signage within the space, accessible travel plans, programming, and attitudinal.

- **Website accessibility and communication** – can you give examples where inclusive programmes were signposted effectively?
- **Physical access considerations** – can you give examples where this was both signposted and effectively supported your experience?
- **Signage within the space** – can you give some examples of how and in what way this supported your visit?
- **Accessible travel plans** – can you give an example when travel to the venue was effectively communicated by the organisation and how this supported your experience?
- **Programming** – can you give an example of effective inclusive programming?
- **Attitudinal** – can you give example of where staff were friendly, welcoming and had training and this was clear in their manner and actions and how this supported your visit?

Advice to organisations

- In terms of access to arts and culture, what are the key principles that you would like cultural organisations to adopt and what advice would you give to help them meet those goals?

  Meet the parents, a profile of parent activists

It's time the arts stood up for and found ways of representing the complex and all too human experience of this forgotten minority.

Stephen Unwin
(Taken from his website, www.stephenunwin.uk)

Stephen Unwin, father to Joey

Stephen Unwin is an established theatre director, writer, and the father of Joey, a young man with severe learning difficulties. Joey is nonverbal and needs support for day-to-day activities. Joey also has epilepsy and needs 24-hour care.

Image 5.1 Stephen Unwin and Joey
Source: Courtesy of Stephen Unwin

Stephen has considerable experience and expertise in the space of arts, culture, and inclusion. He has written several books and a play exploring how people who have special educational needs have been portrayed in literature and how they have been treated historically. He is also the chair of the charity KIDS, which provides a range of services to disabled children, young people, and their families. Stephen has also written a manifesto that gives guidance on how to write about people with learning disabilities.

Writing

In his play *All Our Children*, Stephen exposes how representation historically has led to cruel and dehumanising behaviour. The play, set against the eugenics of the Second World War, explores how people with disabilities were treated. This is one example of Stephen's work in this space and his exploration of representation and language that constructs identities.

Twitter

Stephen is an avid tweeter and uses his platform to challenge preconceptions around disabled people with a particular focus on challenging the tragedy model of disability. He posts images on Twitter that shows the joy of being a parent with a learning-disabled son and how the privilege of being his farther has been an education and enriched his life.

The tragedy model

The tragedy model of disability, as with the medical model, views disability as a deficit. Within this model disability is something that has to be endured, struggled with, and overcome. It supports the notion of ableism and normalcy.

Fighting the system

Stephen also talks openly about his experiences and the challenges, not of his son, but of the systems that should be supporting Joey and how navigating them are exhausting. These systems view disability as a deficit, which is a common experience for parents of disabled children. The systems that are in place to support people with disabilities are means tested. You need to emphasise your disability in order to access the care and support needed. Parents and carers have to describe in very negative terms what their child cannot do. The system is in itself abusive. The process is uninclusive and is very much rooted in the medical model of disability where the deficit is located within the person. It doesn't ask what support you need; it asks what is wrong with you.

A hierarchy in inclusion?

Stephen's view of this space is informed by his own experiences and that of his son Joey. During our conversation we discuss the notion of advocacy within the space of arts, culture, and inclusion. Within the space of inclusion some voices can be heard louder than others and this can be problematic. There is limited 'oxygen' and this can mean that some voices are heard while others aren't. In Joey's case, given that he is nonverbal, Stephen is his voice. He is concerned that this might lead to a hierarchy within the space of advocacy where those who can't self-advocate are silent, and that self-advocacy privileges the most articulate.

Running a commercial arts organisation and the benefits and tensions of inclusion

Stephen was the artistic director of the Rose Theatre in Kingston. During our conversation we discuss the logistics and organisational factors that theatres need to accommodate if they are to include disabled actors in a meaningful way. Structures need to have 'flex' in order to make sure that they include disabled actors and facilitate their process. Systems for rehearsals need to be inclusive so that they work for disabled actors. It's important to understand that it's not only about physical access; it is also attitudinal and structural.

Cultural organisations as community assets

Cultural spaces are also community assets. In addition to being spaces where culture is lived and experienced, they are also places where people meet and can give communities a sense of place and identity. Bars and cafés within these spaces can be meeting places for the whole community. All these spaces can be mapped as an inclusive exercise and opportunities signposted and experienced in a number of meaningful ways. This offers the opportunity to build a diverse community where people can come together for different reasons and purposes but are seen and valued within the same space. This approach would increase organisations' scope and understanding of inclusion. It would be a long-term initiative and would need to be a strategically driven and supported in policy for it to be real and sustainable.

Inclusive programming

Stephen described his experience of programming within a commercial theatre and some of the tensions that exist within this space. For inclusion to be both meaningful and sustainable, it needs to be structural. It needs to be mapped effectively with opportunities signposted and delivered. It needs to be within a sustainable financial model. It needs to be outward looking and promoted extensively. What is good for the theatre is good for the whole community, and it is crucial that this is acknowledged and valued.

Writing about people with learning disabilities. A manifesto by Stephen Unwin

1. Stories with characters with learning disabilities who aren't defined solely by their learning disabilities.
2. Stories in which, when a character's learning disabilities are mentioned, we see the social structures surrounding him or her.
3. Stories which recognize the challenges of a relative with learning disabilities, but don't show them simply as a tragedy.
4. Stories of people with learning disabilities which aren't simply examples of courage in the face of insuperable odds.
5. Stories in which people with learning disabilities aren't granted special powers or abilities.
6. Stories which don't expect people with learning disabilities to convey a load of metaphorical meanings.
7. Stories in which family members can be shown to be frustrated by their relative's learning disabilities while also loving them forever.
8. Stories which show that while people with learning disabilities are sometimes the victims of abuse and cruelty, they often bring out the very best in the people who come into contact with them.
9. Stories which show the funny side of some learning-disabled behaviour without falling into contempt or abuse.
10. Stories in which the language of contempt and abuse towards people with learning disabilities is challenged.

Lisha Rooney

Lisha Rooney is the mother of a child with autism and owner of WhatDo, a company that makes sensory-friendly, carbon-neutral, diversity-positive clothing. Lisha is a school governor and has an MA in fine arts. Lisha has also presented at the Cultural Inclusion Manifesto Conferences and is an ambassador for the Flute Theatre Company.

Image 5.2 Lisha and Lumen
Source: Courtesy of Lisha Rooney

Visibility and representation

What are your views on representation; do you feel there are any examples where disability has been portrayed in a way that is relatable?

'My experience of any representation in mainstream media – television series, films, news, and radio – is that it is nonrelatable. There is only one programme over the last couple of years that stands out as somewhat relatable (and even that was not completely relatable): *Harvey and Me* on BBC1, the documentary on Katie Price navigating care and education for her autistic son Harvey Price. There do seem to be more books being published (some self-published or published by educational publishers) that are more relatable.

'I tend to find more relatable representations on social media, but even then, they are not completely relatable. Most of the accounts and groups I follow or am a member of are autistic-led, which is extremely helpful, but not always relatable from the perspective of a parent who is not autistic. I can still relate – based on my observations of my own autistic son – to their experiences and depictions of stimming, experiences of meltdowns, experiences within social situations, medical diagnosis and healthcare, therapies, educations, and so many other topics'.

What do you think are characteristics of inclusive authentic portrayal?

'Inclusive authentic portrayal manages to not depict any shame or embarrassment while simultaneously not being exploitive. We can see ear defenders, augmentative and alternative communication (AAC) chewelry, chewy and fidget toys, soft toys and other comfort items, bare feet, various stims (jumping, flapping, stimming, voice stims), without any negativity, judgment, or apology. I feel in order for it to be sincere and honest, it has to be a lived experience and not an actor's portrayal'.

Can you describe why it is important to be authentically portrayed?

'If autistic individuals are not authentically portrayed, acceptance will never happen. If actions, behaviours, or aspects of personalities are hidden or sugar-coated, this leaves no space for acceptance or a celebration of difference. As we witnessed in the film *Music* (which I refuse to watch on moral grounds), created by Sia. Unless someone – or a condition – is authentically portrayed, it often becomes a depiction of a stereotype, and ultimately, exploitive, patronising, offensive, and harmful for a community which already has to try so hard to live in a world not tailored to its needs. Portrayals of autistic individuals by directors, producers, writers, and other creators as lacking or other or unworthy demean the entire autistic community.

'True portrayals should show understanding and compassion for and hopefully incorporate actual, lived experience – the individuals represented, and I'm not sure abled individuals can ever create truly authentic works using only abled individuals to depict a disabled individual's experience. What often happens – in such films as *Rain Man* or *My Left Foot* – is the story says less about the disabled individual and more about everyone else's idea, judgment, or fear of him/her. If someone approached me about making a film about my autistic son Lumen, and asked if an actor near to his age could shadow him to learn more about him and his ways, my first instinct would be to ask the filmmaker why he/she would not cast my son. And then I would ask him/her to really reflect on his/her answer'.

Access

Website accessibility and communication: can you give examples where inclusive programmes were signposted effectively?

'Generally, inclusive programmes – if offered at all – are still not signposted effectively and are difficult to find on websites. I often subscribe to any education or access newsletter available, and the information is more forthcoming and easier to navigate in the email. My first search is usually in the "Visit" section, and there I look for any "Access" information. Royal Academy is fantastic in both their offerings and effectiveness. They have a comprehensive section on their site, inclusive for several disabilities and conditions. They offer downloadable sensory maps and visual stories, as well a phone number and email if you require a short sensory synopsis of an exhibition that doesn't feature a relaxed opening. They list their upcoming relaxed openings and quiet zone events and allow site visitors to subscribe to access-related emails'.

Physical access considerations: can you give examples where this was both signposted and effectively supported your experience?

'Physical access considerations usually come in the form of relaxed openings, where the entire venue makes adjustments in the form of less visitors, lights dimmed, no music, hand dryers turned off, and the offering of a quiet/sensory space. This has been signposted in the email invite to such events, and then related by staff at the entrance of the event, when they hand out literature and a map. This has happened at the Science Museum, Natural History Museum, Tower Bridge, the Transport Museum, and at an event at the Saatchi Gallery'.

Signage within the space: can you give some examples of how and in what way this supported your visit?

'I have only ever seen signage in the actual space during relaxed openings, and the signage indicated where the quiet/sensory space was. I am yet to see any signage at non-relaxed events, or signage which indicates where toilets without hand dryers are (or are turned off). There is only one cultural institution – Royal Academy – with signage available on the printed sensory maps. All other cultural institutions maps we've seen have no indication of any quiet/sensory space or toilets without hand dryers, and it is likely because they are not offered'.

Accessible travel plans: can you give an example when travel to the venue was effectively communicated by the organisation and how this supported your experience?

'There are generally no considerations for disabled travel to venues, including autistic individuals traveling. We have always navigated travel ourselves and taken either public transport or a taxi to various cultural institutions. As we will soon have a car and my son is eligible for a blue badge, I have only recently started researching parking. Certain venues, including Tate Modern, allow us to book accessible parking by emailing or calling and relating relevant information – name, contact details, car registration number, and date and time of visit'.

Advice to organisations

In terms of access to arts and culture, what are the key principles that you would like cultural organisations to adopt and what advice would you give to help them meet those goals?

'It is paramount and necessary for cultural institutions to understand that, if they are not being inclusive, they are actively excluding. By not being inclusive, cultural institutions are conveying to autistic individuals that they're not worth it.

'Being treated like "other" – there are the "usual" visitors and there are "other" visitors – insinuates a stance of superiority, lack of respect for difference, and a refusal to accept. Cultural inclusion needs to be understood institution-wide, from trustees to invigilators. Ideally, such understanding would come in the form of actually spending time with autistic individuals. This would allow for the understanding and acceptance of common autistic behaviours, such as flapping, jumping, spinning, running, talking when everyone else is silent, wearing ear defenders, wearing no shoes, chewing on items or clothing, or experiencing sensory overload. Rather than unsettle the autistic individual or his/her parent or carer by making irrational demands, staff could revel in the sincerity, the spontaneity – both emotional and physiological – of distinct reactions art elicits amongst autistic individuals and allow certain non-harmful and non-disruptive behaviours without interjecting.

'Ideal conditions for viewing art and reactions provoked by works and are not one-size-fits-all scenarios and can be very different for neurotypical and autistic viewers. Considering art's subjective nature, cultural institutions should not require particular viewing parameters or responses which are more concealed or confined to the countenance. I understand not wanting viewers on the floor sprawled out in snow angel position or mimicking whirling dervishes across the perimeter, but autistic individuals and/or we parents and carers are aware a museum is not a park, a dance studio, or a playground. We are also cognisant of health and safety issues and the justified fear of works being damaged. Autistic individuals' responses to artworks, their communication and regulation in the form of different behaviours are just that: responses, communication and regulation. There is no malice, and actions are not intended to disrupt, frighten or anger gallery assistants, invigilators or fellow visitors.

'Understanding and acceptance might also allow staff to make exceptions when autistic individuals are unable to follow set routes, which have become more common since lockdown. Or to queue separately for bag searches and exhibition entrances, as this impatience often prevents even entering the cultural institution'.

April Li

April Li is the mother of Mia. April developed the Portraits of Grit Instagram feed that 'Raises disability awareness through telling everyday stories of trials and triumphs'. April has also presented at the Cultural Inclusion Manifesto Conference on her work in this space.

Visibility and representation

What are your views on representation; do you feel there are any examples where disability has been portrayed in a way that is relatable?

'My sense of disability representation looking back from childhood until now is that there may have been progress in terms of greater visibility and awareness of people with different needs (although caveat that I think this is more

Image 5.3 April and Mia
Source: Courtesy of April Li

in the realm of visible disabilities) but actual representation is still very poor, whether that be in positions of power (government, board rooms etc.), in the workforce or in media in general.

'I think all too often disability is framed in terms of stereotypes. Disabled people are seen either as an object of pity (as needing charity or as a drain on public funds) or to be marvelled at as an inspiration for "overcoming the odds" or having succeeded "in spite of" his/her disability. None of these perspectives are helpful or representative for most disabled people and has the effect of elevating disability to being some type of personality trait, which it is not. Ask anyone that has lived experiences of disability and one of the first things they will probably tell you is that they don't wish to be defined by their disability, and yet here we are doing precisely that whenever they are mentioned (whether in a positive or negative light).

'In terms of portrayal of disability, I think there are certainly elements of different programmes that I have seen that have portrayed disability in a way that I feel is fairly relatable. I'm thinking – *The A Word* or *There She Goes* – both dramas that were on BBC. The other one that springs to mind is *Dangerous Giant Animals*, a play that was written and performed by Christina Murdock (it's an autobiography about disability from a sibling perspective)'.

What do you think are characteristics of inclusive authentic portrayal?

'I think portrayal by a disabled actor is a start as well as contribution from people with lived experiences of disability to the creative process to ensure authenticity. In general, I would just say it's about authenticity and that should permeate through all processes that relate to the portrayal – be it casting, creative process, background research etc. Can you describe why it is important to be authentically portrayed? Goodness – where to start! I think it's good for well-being for a start. For those who are the subject of the portrayal, it is easier to relate and connect and empowers those individuals. I think storytelling is incredibly important – whether they are positive or negative stories – it's important that they get told.

For the individual being portrayed, it is empowering as it helps to make people feel relevant and may inspire them. It's just like from a gender perspective, it's often talked about how it's important to have role models and see women in positions of power in the workplace. It's no different here. For others, it educates and builds empathy, broadening perspectives. I think there is enormous power in sharing authentic stories as a way of shifting perspectives. As an educational tool, I think it is particularly important in the context of educating the younger generation. Teaching kids that every voice matters. So, in short, authentic portrayal is a force for good and contributes to a better more empathetic society and so from my perspective should be seen as a social obligation to help shift negative attitudes towards disability. At a very basic level, it helps to generate opportunities for the portrayal itself to be a talking point. I think all too often there is this awkwardness around talking about disability (and that extends to those who are living with disability themselves). Having authentic portrayals would help normalise disability or at least generate conversations around it. If it isn't even portrayed (let alone authentically portrayed), it is less likely to be talked about!'

Access

Website accessibility and communication: can you give examples where inclusive programmes were signposted effectively?

'I think my experience is that inclusive programmes are rarely obviously signposted. I can't think of anything I have experienced that didn't involve either someone telling me about it or me digging around to look for it. Sometimes, I've called up to find out and I find that once I speak to someone, they are usually very helpful. It's just that the information is not that readily accessible online (other than general accessibility statements which don't always provide the detail you want)'.

Physical access considerations: can you give examples where this was both signposted and effectively supported your experience?

'My experience is that once you get access to something – e.g. getting on an access list – then you get lots of helpful information. Otherwise, it's not really that clearly signposted and it's easier to just call up and ask.

'The place that I hold out to be the best example of being inclusive and accessible is probably the Bridge Theatre. It's always more comforting to go somewhere that you have been before so you know what to expect, but the Bridge Theatre stands out as the one place where I felt totally welcome and 100% prepared even before our first visit there. I joined the access list and then got an email back from someone where they asked me a whole host of questions. It took some time to fill in but that in itself made me feel like they were genuinely interested to know. It was things like trying to understand what our needs were so that it could be smoother the next time we visited'.

Signage within the space: can you give some examples of how and in what way this supported your visit?

'Most places that are in modern buildings I feel now are quite good at signage – mainly where the loos are. A standout example would probably be the Royal Academy's sensory map'.

Accessible travel plans: can you give an example when travel to the venue was effectively communicated by the organisation and how this supported your experience?

'It wasn't relevant to us as we were not driving but, prior to attending, the Bridge Theatre gave us details of the exact closest streets (and a map) where there were parking spots for blue badge holders (including the number of spots at each location). I imagine this would have been incredibly useful for someone who was driving and had a blue badge'.

Programming: can you give an example of effective inclusive programming?

'Unicorn Theatre always seems to provide social stories and even those aren't necessarily always easily understandable for Mia, it helps me to know so that I can explain it to her/tell her about it in a way that I think she'll understand. Performances put on by Oily Cart also do great social stories and tend to be more visual stories that are very helpful'.

Attitudinal: can you give example of where staff were friendly, welcoming and had training and this was clear in their manner and actions and how this supported your visit?

'I have thought long and hard about this and I'm afraid I can't think of many examples. Not because people are unwelcoming but just that we've not really had cause to test this. I think part of it is that Mia's disability is not really visible so I guess I feel like often it's not obvious that we may need help.

'I do recall there was an occasion at the Welcome Collection when one of the staff came up to me and Mia and tried to engage Mia in conversation. I probably stepped in feeling a bit conscious that Mia probably wouldn't respond with something polite. This happens often I think when people are just trying to be nice, but on this occasion, the staff member noticeably changed how she approached Mia. Usually people just keep asking questions (probably to see if they can find a different way to engage) or make comments about how she must be shy. This lady instead I think tried to show her how she would engage with an exhibit – she sort of stopped asking questions and touched an exhibit that was particularly tactile and encouraged Mia to do the same. I don't recall if it changed anything in Mia, but I just remember feeling relieved and grateful for the kindness she showed. I have no idea if she was trained at all, but she clearly read Mia very well'.

Advice to organisations

In terms of access to arts and culture, what are the key principles that you would like cultural organisations to adopt and what advice would you give to help them meet those goals?

'To me, access is about getting in. All too often (especially in London) I feel like the main problem is that people can't even get in in the first place whether that is because of prohibitive cost, fears of the unknown, not knowing how it might affect or accommodate people with specific needs.

So, in terms of advice, it would be broad principles like – arts and culture shouldn't be just for the middle class or for the able-bodied or the neurotypical!

I feel people with disabilities should have preferential access to everything! Arts and cultural establishments should have a block of reserved tickets for people with disabilities. Even better if a proportion could be free. I have spoken to so many parents who just don't bother because they think their child would only last a short period of time – how amazing if those families were not denied even if they can only last half an hour or whatever it is or even more amazing if their child surprises them and ends up loving it. That is an untapped opportunity that could be a really unexpectedly positive experience for someone.

That aside, I think a really simple thing that everyone could do is to just say at the point of booking – if you have a disability – tell us! They could then point you towards what seats might be best depending on your needs, or what aspects of the show/exhibit might be challenging, general info about accessibility – all of this is simple information that people could receive upfront (the team could just be given a crib sheet with the relevant details) and I am sure that simple gesture would go a really long way to make people feel more welcomed from the get go.

I recognise that it's difficult to be all things to all people but I think there are some basic things (like accessible website or appropriate signage or advance information about the program) which should be offered and having something like what I suggest above at the booking stage just conveys an attitude of awareness and would be massively appreciated'.

Claire Madge

Claire is the mother of two children with a diagnosis of autism. She runs the Autism in Museums website and is a museum blogger where she writes about exhibitions and volunteering. Claire is currently the blogger in residence at the Cartoon Museum in London and sits on the London & South Committee of the National Lottery Heritage Fund.

Image 5.4 Claire Madge and her daughter Bella

Source: Courtesy of Claire Madge

Visibility and representation

What are your views on representation; do you feel there are any examples where you feel that disability has been portrayed in a way that you feel is relatable?

'As autism is a spectrum, finding something that is "relatable" can be hard. I feel sometimes that *The Curious Incident of the Dog in the Night-Time* (which I still haven't read) is our generation's *Rain Man* in the sense that everyone tells me I should see the play and read the book. I don't think there can be one film or book that tells the story of autism. As I mentioned to you it has been more important to me as my daughter has grown up and seeks her own understanding of who she is. When she was 10, I used CBBC Rosie King's *My Autism and Me* as a way to start the conversation.

I thought *The A Word* was good, but I couldn't bear to watch most of it because it was too close to home. I don't think any film or TV programme is going to give you a truly relatable experience as it is a fictionalised version of life. I recently read *How to Be Autistic* by Charlotte Amelia Poe and I think there are much more autistic people getting their voices out there which helps capture the individuality of autism. A couple of years ago I read *NeuroTribes* by Steve Silberman, which I think really set the history of autism and diagnosis into context for me. The portrayal of a non-verbal autistic girl of colour in Pixar's *Loop* is also a moment and a cultural move forward'.

What do you think are characteristics of inclusive authentic portrayal?

'You have to speak to and work with autistic people/actors to really represent what it means to be autistic. Not just one voice but understanding different experiences. An authentic portrayal shows the good and the bad, the highs and the lows, because that is life'.

Can you describe why it is important to be authentically portrayed?

'It is has become more important to me as my daughter has grown up. She is 17 now and those portrayals affect how she sees herself and how other people see her. People believe what they see, they don't often question the media so having authentic portrayals helps spread awareness and understanding. Society needs to understand the impacts of learning disabilities and autism to prevent mistreatment of autistic people as we have seen in the news'.

Access

Website accessibility and communication: can you give examples where inclusive programmes were signposted effectively?

'The State of Museum Access Survey 2018 which I worked on with VocalEyes and StageText really highlighted the lack of access information on websites and give guidance about how to improve. I think this work has helped highlight how important it is.

'One of the best websites I have seen is the Met in New York who have a whole page dedicated to autism information and resources. The Museum of English Rural Life are very good with BSL is British Sign Language video welcome, visual story, sensory map and Google Street Tour. It is about offering information in different formats so it can work for a wide range of people. Why does this information even have to sit under access or accessibility? Shouldn't it just be welcome information as it helps lots of visitors who might not think they have a disability?

'I like to see visual stories and sensory maps on museum websites; it shows they have thought about their environment and are aware of sensory sensitivities. Covid has brought into sharp relief how anxious many visitors are about the new rules and routines. Many visual stories and welcome videos are being produced to welcome visitors back to museums. Hull Museums have Covid visual stories and an easy read guide to ticketing which is brilliant'.

Physical access considerations: can you give examples where this was both signposted and effectively supported your experience?

'We don't have physical access needs but one daughter struggles with lifts and anxiety and my youngest son can find spiral staircases and glass staircases problematic. It is important to have options and to know what to expect when we visit. It is more about flexibility for us, so being able to book end of the row at the theatre can alleviate a lot of stress and is a simple thing. Being able to skip queues as anxiety builds whilst waiting. At the British Museum when we ran the first Morning Explorers event, we realised the exit and getting families out of the building was problematic as the building got busier. In that instance it was about letting families know about the back exit to the museum which is often quieter. Knowing there is a chill-out space or quiet room is also helpful'.

Signage within the space: can you give some examples of how and in what way this supported your visit?

'At autism early openings extra signage can be helpful to know what areas of the museum are open and closed, where the cloak room is etc. They often have the timing sessions of activities really clearly displayed so that we know when activities are beginning and ending. Just simple things that can help plan and prepare with a child who is autistic. Many autistic visitors can be anxious if they don't know how long an exhibition is or which way to go round so having extra signage and arrows can help. Ironically Covid one-way routes can be beneficial as they help navigate unfamiliar spaces. Most relaxed openings have visual stories and maps handed out on the day or sent beforehand; this can help prepare visitors and help navigating on the day'.

Accessible travel plans: can you give an example when travel to the venue was effectively communicated by the organisation and how this supported your experience?

'I can't think of specific times when we have visited and we have been given this info. We are sometimes in a visual story given info about the nearest train/tube stops. It was interesting that for some families coming to the British Museum on a Sunday for their morning explorer events they had to drive because there weren't any trains that early in the morning. I always encourage museums where possible to see if there are planned tube strikes or engineering works to warn families in advance. At the British Museum for the visual story, we highlighted free parking near the museum. Particularly with anxiety about travelling on public transport post-Covid highlighting accessible parking can be very beneficial'.

Programming: can you give an example of effective inclusive programming?

'Lots of museums run early and relaxed programming – Natural History Museum Dawnosaurs, Science Museum Early Birds, Jewish Museum Curious Explorers, London Transport Museum Morning Explorers etc. We have been to relaxed performances at the Globe, National Theatre, and English National Opera. London Transport Museum is good because they listened to feedback and offered an after-hours event to give families choice of when to attend.

'Many families push back on the idea of only being able to attend at "special times" while some find it easier as they know that there is a lack of judgement from other families who understand the difficulties.

'I think good inclusive programming offers a tiered approach – relaxed openings at different times, support in regular hours (training/visual story/quiet rooms) and more bespoke offers for families with greater need – e.g. Royal Academy art SEN sessions. Whatever is done – making it regular and putting dates up early makes a big difference for families. Not many do this – London Transport Museum just put 4/5 dates up for the rest of the year, this helps families plan'.

Attitudinal: can you give example of where staff were friendly, welcoming and had training and this was clear in their manner and actions and how this supported your visit?

'I asked my husband about this as I find it difficult when I have been working lots of places, I often know they have training. He said it was obvious that the Science Museum had really good awareness because you didn't have to wear a wrist band for the Early Birds events (our daughter doesn't like physical things that feel different). The welcome is always really good, but we don't feel like we are being followed round. Also, the British Museum event as they explained clearly what you could do and see and gave you supporting material to help on your visit.

'I am very impressed with the Postal Museum, which has a strong relationship with the charity Ambitious About Autism. The Youth Panel have helped them plan events and resources; they have also volunteered at their "Post Early" openings. Having young autistic adults volunteer at events is really inspirational for young autistic visitors.

'The Science Museum also ran Night Owls events for young adults with the Ambitious About Autism youth panel and got them in early to help prepare them for the session. I think it shows engagement on another level when organisations are working with autism charities on a long-term basis'.

Advice to organisations

In terms of access to arts and culture, what are the key principles that you would like cultural organisations to adopt and what advice would you give to help them meet those goals?

'A holistic approach is so important. I spoke to the Autograph Gallery who had training from Touretteshero and they said the training was for all staff; they said it was transformational in their approach to how they work and the audiences they welcome.

'Pre-visit information, whether that is sensory maps/visual stories or welcome videos, supports many different types of visitors. It shows awareness of the sensory sensitivities that visitors might have.

'Programming needs to be flexible and tiered as I mentioned earlier. Advice would be – training and awareness is key for all and doesn't have to cost a fortune. Funding from the core rather than an add-on would make a big difference. It is not just about families and children but adults too. Many autism events just cater for younger audiences. I think it is really important to share and celebrate the good work that is done. That shared learning/inspiration is fundamental to change across the sector'.

Cultural implications

Cultural organisations with good practice

Cultural organisation	Inclusive programming mentioned
The Museum of English Rural Life	BSL video welcome video, sensory map, and Google tour
Royal Academy of Arts	Downloadable sensory maps, visual stories, a short sensory synopsis of an exhibition, and SEN sessions
Hull Museum	Easy read ticketing guide and visual story
Natural History Museum	Dawnosaurs: relaxed programming
Science Museum	Early Birds: relaxed programming and Night Owls – working with Ambitious About Autism
Jewish Museum	Curious Explorers: relaxed programming
London Transport Museum	Morning Explorers: relaxed programming
British Museum	Morning Explorer: relaxed opening
Globe Theatre	Relaxed performances
National Theatre	Relaxed performances
English National Opera	Relaxed performances
Bridge Theatre	Access mailing list available
Unicorn Theatre	Social stories available
Oily Cart	Social stories available
Postal Museum	Ambitious About Autism – the Youth Panel have helped them plan events and resources; they have also volunteered at their 'Post Early' openings
Metropolitan Museum	Website page dedicated to autism information and resources

Other cultural organisations mentioned

Autograph Gallery
Tower Bridge
The Saatchi Gallery
Welcome Collection

Summary of key points

The focus of this chapter was to give voice and emphasise the centrality of families to the notion of inclusion within arts and culture. Through these interviews a commonality of experiences has emerged.

- Portrayal of disability by a disabled actor is crucial as is consulting widely with those who have lived experience throughout the whole creative process
- Authentic portrayal of disability provides much needed role models for disabled children and young people as well as raising awareness
- It is an excellent idea for cultural organisations to develop mutually beneficial partnerships with disability charities. Such collaborations can improve organisations' offers as well as provide work experiences for disabled young people
- An effective way for cultural organisations to develop their understanding of disabled visitors' needs is to spend time with them
- It's important to understand that it's not only about physical access; it is also attitudinal and structural
- Cultural spaces are also community assets. In addition to being spaces where culture is lived and experienced, they are also places where people meet and can give communities a sense of place and identity
- What is good for cultural organisations is good for the whole community, and it is crucial that this is acknowledged and valued
- For inclusion to be meaningful and sustainable it needs to be structural and sit within an organisation's financial framework

- There is a lot to do to ensure that websites are fully inclusive, but there are some excellent examples of good practice to draw on in this chapter
- Providing high-quality information and signposting for disabled people enhances the experience for everyone
- Good inclusive programming offers a tiered approach, including relaxed openings at different times, support in regular hours (training/visual story/quiet rooms), and more bespoke offers for families with greater needs

Educational implications

Families are central to the educational success of their child. They are critical to the development of their education health care (EHC) plans and how the provision is organised. Anecdotal and research evidence shows that the more that families are involved in the school community, the better they can directly support their child in making progress. Schools are community hubs and places where parents can access and be signposted to other services. Schools are highly skilled at brokering partnerships, and this can also translate to accessing local cultural organisations. When I coordinated the West London Inclusive Arts Festival, we actively developed a strand to include parents. If you wanted to work effectively within this space it is important to engage families, listen to their needs, and build relationships so that you can effectively co-produce opportunities. Ways in which you can do this include the following:

Ensure that you invite parents to your sharing and celebrating activities and events

We noticed a significant increase in parental attendance throughout the school when parents were invited to a range of events across the school year. It does need support and requires planning so that invites are sent at different intervals and in different formats to ensure effective communication. It is definitely worth the effort.

Include parents into festivals/schools' activities

This can be as separate parents/families strands or they might want to co-lead an activity if they have a skill that they would like to share. One of our partner schools organised a crèche on days when activities were happening in school so parents could then spend time with their other children at the school. Before moving to action, spend time finding out the needs of your parents.

Act as a broker with local cultural organisations

We organised a coffee and cake morning at the Royal Albert Hall and invited parents along to meet their education team. The informal and relaxed atmosphere allowed people to get to know and understand each other's needs. It can be a great opportunity to then move to action, which might mean that you support a cultural partner with organising a focus group or publicising their programming through the school's communication networks. This highlights the importance of developing local cultural networks and building mutually beneficial relationships with organisations.

Arrange art activities to facilitate parent groups

We also arranged coffee mornings with our parent's group in the art room. We would make the art teacher, and a range of materials, available and people were given the option of engaging in art activities if they wanted. These were very successful, and the number of parents who attended increased significantly.

Key points

- Plan your calendar of events and activities and ensure that you communicate this effectively to parents and families in a range of formats.
- Organise parent steering groups to find out their needs and what they would like to do; remember this may take time, but it is crucial to invest in developing relationships before moving to action.
- Think laterally about how to accommodate parent's needs. An example is providing a crèche for their other children, which is a creative way of increasing their engagement with their disabled child and the particular activity you are promoting.
- Act as a broker with your cultural partners in your local area; organise a *getting to know you* meeting.

- Build meaningful and mutually beneficial relationships with a range of local arts and cultural organisations to increase opportunities for the children and young people you work with while improving the offer available to all disabled people in your area.
- Organise coffee mornings and use art activities to facilitate and support relationships.

Concluding notes

The importance of families is central to inclusion. It was very important that in a book that looked at supporting inclusion within arts and culture that the parent's voice was heard. Practical examples of this are explored throughout this book in chapter 10, and a parental view was part of the conversation that describes culturally inclusive schools in chapter 13.

Further reading

Plays

All Our Children, about the Nazi persecution of disabled children, was premiered at Jermyn Street Theatre in London in 2017. It received its US premiere in 2019 at the Sheen Centre in New York.

Website

More information on Stephen's work can be found at www.stephenunwin.uk

Twitter handle

@RoseUnwin

Further reading

Lisha recommends this website: www.notanautismmom.com

Key points

Television

- *The A Word* (BBC)
- *There She Goes* (BBC)

Plays

- *Dangerous Giant Animals* by Christina Murdock

Autism in museums is the website that Claire runs that shares all the information on accessible programming

Television

- *My Autism and Me* – CBBC
- *Loop* – portrayal of a nonverbal autistic girl

Books

- *How to Be Autistic* by Charlotte Amelia Page
- *NeuroTribes* by Steve Silberman

Website accessibility

- The State of Museums Access Survey 2018
- VocalEyes: experience art and culture through audio description. www.vocaleyes.co.uk
- StageText: making theatre and culture accessible to deaf, deafened, and hard of hearing people. www.stagetext.org

6 Producers of art and culture

Disabled-focused and disabled-led organisations

This chapter profiles four organisations that are either disabled focused or disabled led and considers their artistic vision and body of work in relation to activism. It explores these organisations' approaches to working in this space, considers the idea of **role models** through a conversation with DJ, a dancer with Corali Dance Company, and promotes the concept of the **inclusive canon**.

The chapter looks at how disabled-led and disabled-focused organisations can help a school to develop a rich and inclusive approach to employment routes and support their compliance with the **Gatsby benchmarks**. It also demonstrates how you can embed these organisations within the structure of the **Arts Award qualification**. Finally, the chapter has an interview with Jennifer Gilbert of the Jennifer Lauren Gallery, the most prominent gallery that supports and showcases D/deaf, disabled, and neurodivergent artists.

How to use this chapter

At the end of the chapter there is signposting to these organisations and a summary of key points and references to **Gatsby benchmark number 5**.

The inclusive canon: why is this important?

It is fundamental that disabled artists are 'seen' in society so that young disabled people see themselves reflected as producers of culture and can see a career trajectory within arts and culture.

It is also important that all artists are acknowledged and that they reflect society in the broadest sense. Arts and culture is a space that can challenge preconceptions through storytelling and activism and is an important place for shaping our society and its values.

The idea of an **inclusive canon** is very timely. In the introductory chapter the idea of visibility and value were discussed in chapter 3, which explores cultural inclusion and cultural capital from an educational perspective, raises both concerns and lays down a challenge, a challenge that the inclusive canon seeks to meet!

History of art and activism

The trajectory and timeline of activism within arts and culture is described by the **National Disability Arts Collection and Archive**. I've distilled the information presented on their website into a timeline to contextualise the trajectory of this movement.

This timeline gives you an overview of how the movement towards greater inclusion was spearheaded by arts and culture and a sense of trajectory to the present day.

This chapter focuses on four organisations

- Drake Music
- ActionSpace
- Corali Dance Company
- Graeae Theatre Company
- Jennifer Lauren Gallery

What are the Gatsby benchmarks?

For the purposes of this chapter, we will briefly explore what the Gatsby benchmarks are with particular focus on **benchmark number 5**. One of the drivers of the Gatsby benchmark is a holistic and strategic approach to supporting young people's access to high-quality career guidance.

DOI: 10.4324/9781003122258-6

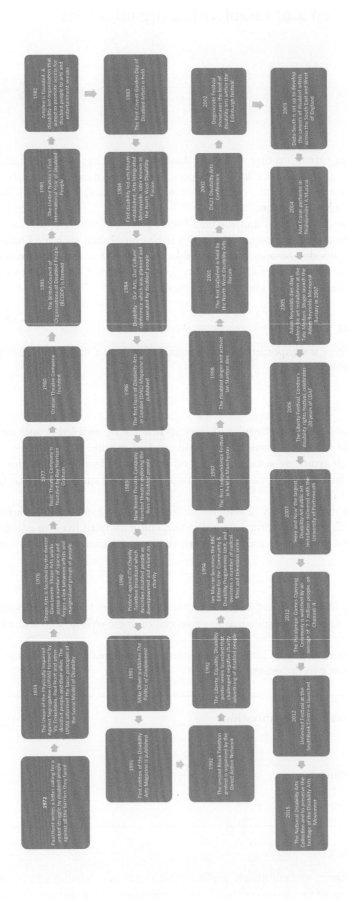

The eight Gatsby benchmarks of Good Career Guidance are:

1. A stable careers programme
2. Learning from career and labour market information
3. Addressing the needs of each pupil
4. Linking curriculum learning to careers
5. Encounters with employers and employees
6. Experiences of workplaces
7. Encounters with further and higher education
8. Personal guidance

Drake Music

Image 6.1 Drake Music logo

Drake Music is the leading national organisation working in music, disability, and technology. They have been in this space for over 20 years and work nationally across the whole of the UK. It is a National Portfolio Organisation for Arts Council England and is funded through Youth Music, a national music charity.

⋆ **National Portfolio Organisations** are leaders in their areas, with a collective responsibility to protect and develop our national arts and cultural ecology. (Taken from the Relationship Framework document; How Arts Council England works with National Portfolio Organisations, 2018–2022).

Drake Music's vision

> is a world where disabled people have the same range of opportunities, instruments and encouragement, where disabled and non-disabled musicians work together as equals.

(Taken from Drake Music's website)

Drake Music works in this space as a technological specialist to enable more people to make music using technology to break down barriers. Drake Music is a disability-focused organisation, working with disabled people of all ages from schoolchildren to disabled musicians and believes in equity of access and representation. This is also embedded within the structure and the culture of the organisation so that disabled and nondisabled people work collectively together for change and inclusion.

History; technological inclusion

Founded in the 1980s by Adèle Drake, Drake Research Project – as it was known at that point – looked to use the progress in music technology to include disabled people in the making of music. Technology heralded a new era in music making that could lead to greater accessibility and inclusivity. Historically, music making required a level of physical dexterity; however, technological developments enabled a new, inclusive approach to producing music.

Four things which inform the work of Drake Music:

*   We are always learning, and always sharing what we learn
*   Disabled musicians are at the heart of what we do
*   Our work is underpinned by the social model of disability
*   'Nothing about us without us'

Nothing about us without us

An important slogan from the disability rights movement is 'Nothing about us without us'. The slogan origi-nates from the same titled book *Nothing About Us Without Us: Disability Oppression and Empowerment* by James Charlton. This slogan became a rallying cry, as the slogan implies it 'expresses the conviction of people with disabilities that they know what is best for them' and is firmly located within the social model of disability.

How they work

- Promote innovative technology that makes music fully accessible
- Encourage more people to participate in making music
- Support and develop a culture where disabled and nondisabled artists work together as equals
- Programming that supports disabled musicians to progress their careers
- Training and consultancy for teachers, music hubs, and other organisations

Innovation and agents of change; practical inclusion

Working as agents of change within the field of technology, Drake Music supports new and innovative ways of work-ing. Drake has a focus on developing cheaper, cost-effective music technologies to further decrease and remove bar-riers. Drake Music works with all musicians who identify as disabled, from beginner to professional level in schools, arts, and community settings.

A research and campaigning organisation

Challenging and agitating in the space of art, culture, and inclusion, engaging in research and challenging preconcep-tions, approaches, and orthodoxy, Drake Music engages in the wider conversations to promote inclusion in access, representation, and participation.

ActionSpace

Image 6.2 ActionSpace logo

ActionSpace's vision

> *We aim to make a professional career in the arts a realistic option for artists with learning disabilities who have the talent and ambition to pursue this.*

(Taken from ActionSpace's website)

ActionSpace is a London-based visual arts organisation. They work with learning-disabled artists, creating innovative visual art projects. ActionSpace was launched in the 1960s and was established as a charity in 1984. It is acknowledged as a progressive leader in this space and, like Drake Music, is a National Portfolio Organisation. They have been funded by Arts Council England for 20 years and their work in this space has been acknowledged widely. Action-Space was one of just four organisations based in London to receive uplift in their funding for the years 2018–2022 by the Arts Council.

Partnership working

ActionSpace works with a number of large cultural organisations including the Royal Academy of Arts, Camden Arts Centre and the National Portrait Gallery. Through these partnerships ActionSpace has established a space for learning-disabled artists within the contemporary art scene. They also have a long-standing relationship with Studio Voltaire. Studio Voltaire is a charity that supports and promotes contemporary art practice.

Studio-based practice

ActionSpace operates several studios in London located within larger artist studio complexes. ActionSpace artists attend the studios working alongside artist facilitators who support them in developing their practice in partnership with organisations like Studio Voltaire.

Exhibitions and events

Their exhibition programme operates both as a showcase and for the artists to sell their work. There are also a number of participatory events, engaging the general public and others with learning disabilities by inviting them to join in and explore creativity through co-production and co-construction.

Artist development

This is run in partnership with a range of contemporary art organisations. ActionSpace collaborates with these partners to promote equity of access and works with their individual artists in supporting them to develop relationships within the sector. At present ActionSpace is looking at how best they can support and facilitate the transition for young people from school to studio practice.

Young people's programme

ActionSpace also has a young people's programme which supports young learning-disabled people with their creativity and in developing new skills, providing opportunities to network and build creative communities.

Beyond the Studio

An initiative *Beyond the Studio* responds to the needs and interests of London's learning-disabled community. This initiative is inclusive of those young people with profound and complex learning difficulties. These projects work with a range of partners and collaborators and offer bespoke opportunities where new skills can be learnt, building confidence and transforming lives.

Interview with Sheryll Catto, co-director of ActionSpace

The importance of being included

> We've always been clear that our studios must be in mainstream studio complexes and our artists must be working alongside other artists, and be part of whatever else they're doing, and we do that across all three studios. What we do is support professional practice and individual artists. Each one of our artists does something different, they all do their own thing and it's very much about focusing on them. Looking at what they want to do and developing them individually.

The problem with inclusion

> The concept of disability and the idea of disability is a very big space. The needs of someone who has a physical disability without a learning disability is very different from someone who has a learning disability. I think somewhere within all of this must be an understanding that we're talking about a very diverse group of people.

Inclusion: a dynamic approach

> It's about being person centred; it's being able to say what does this person need at this particular moment in time.

Seeing the art and the artist

> I mean our raison d'être is about supporting professional practice within the visual arts. And it's picking young people up, talented young people up as they come out of college or school. Where they've been able to do art, and suddenly they've got nothing, aside from going to a day centre doing an arts and crafts workshop.

Art for art's sake

Sheryll and I discussed some of the barriers her artists experience around the perception of where art is produced and the 'value' that this then imparts on the work. This is a common theme in lots of discussions around inclusion and cultural value and one that is touched on throughout the book and particularly in the chapter that explores historical exclusion.

Art as a secondary outcome

For disabled people there is often the idea that the art or craft produced is secondary to other functions that the process facilitates and supports. In inclusive education we value the process and there is value in this, but what this can then do is deny the young people and young adult's agency by not acknowledging the outcomes of their creativity. The artistic outcome is seen purely as a vehicle for other things, and this has direct impact on the value that it is ascribed to it by society, that is, the drawings that are produced might be viewed as an afternoon activity where the focus is on social engagement and the artwork is secondary. Very similar outcomes can be produced but in different settings, and by their cultural context and information or the discourse in which they are produced can frame their meaning and value in very different ways.

Outsider art

ActionSpace is part of the **European Outsider Art Association**. The European Outsider Art Association is a pan-European organisation that works in the space called outsider art. The association works collectively to promote and develop the sector. It seeks to influence cultural policy and practice of galleries and museums, studios, educational centres, and media.

Outsider art

Outsider art is a term that generally describes art by self-taught artists. This term is very general in nature and describes art from a wide range of artists from diverse backgrounds, including those that are D/deaf, disabled, and neurodivergent.

There are tensions with this label, one that is explored in the following interview with Jennifer Gilbert of the Jennifer Lauren Gallery.

Jennifer Lauren Gallery

> Through her work Jennifer hopes to: demystify what is regarded as art and who can be an artist; stimulate audiences; and continue to challenge the stigma surrounding this field of art.

(Taken from the Jennifer Lauren Gallery website)

The gallery was formed in 2017 by Jennifer Gilbert. The aim of the gallery is to promote the work of underrepresented artists. Artists that are described as outsider artists have historically been overlooked by mainstream galleries and art history. This broad heading of artists covers those that are disabled and self-taught. The gallery has a roster of international artists and takes part in a number of events including artist talks, pop-ups, art fairs, and collaborations with other galleries.

Interview with Jennifer Gilbert

> Championing self-taught, evolving and overlooked artists from around the world.

(Taken from the Jennifer Lauren Gallery website)

The Jennifer Lauren Gallery is run solely by Jennifer Gilbert.

Jennifer talks passionately about how the value of art is perceived and the way in which artists that she represents are framed. Jennifer describes how artist Thompson Hall 'doesn't understand why no one places value on his work'. Thompson currently has a residence at Autograph in London. An overarching aim of Jennifer's work in this space is to challenge these preconceptions and to create spaces within art organisations and institutions that are inclusive and representative of a range of artists and art practice.

★ Autograph Gallery was established in 1988 and champions the work of artists exploring issues exploring race, social justice, and human rights and is located in central London.

Journey towards artistic autonomy and confidence

Jennifer describes how she goes on a journey with her artists, liaising with them and their support network, which might be their family or organisations such as ActionSpace. Jennifer not only curates the shows of her artist, but she also develops workshops and events that enable her artists acquire the skills for them to lead workshops. Working alongside their peers, this supports the artists in developing these key skills and in discovering their own self-identity as artists.

Artist voice

Jennifer creates spaces where she actively encourages her artists to enter into a creative conversation, cultivating their artist voices through these conversations in a safe place that allows for honesty and creative growth. She facilitates these conversations so that there is space for critical feedback and a sense of community with her artists, supporting their development holistically.

Self-labelling, who I am, how I want to be seen

Jennifer is clear that when she shows work that she is promoting the aesthetics of the work and that the art speaks for itself. How artists describe themselves is their choice. Jennifer describes the importance of this and how these labels can depend on the artist's knowledge of the world and how they choose to self-identify. This chimes with the inclusive notion of personhood and acknowledgement, who I am and how I want to be seen.

Outsider art

Jennifer represents artists from around the world, and there are cultural variations in labelling and the value that these labels have. In Japan the term outsider art is embraced as it has positive cultural implications. In the UK the term is currently being scrutinised as it can be problematic in the way that it suggests difference.

Structural inclusion

Through her high-profile shows and collaborations with blue chip galleries such as Flowers Gallery and Carl Freedman Gallery, Jennifer is making changes in these spaces, enabling them to become more accessible as a consequence of these shows. Jennifer talks about how some of these changes are through raising awareness of physical accessibility, such as signposting and making the ramps obvious to ensure physical access to the space, to curation which allows for wheelchairs to move easily through the space and a range of accessible texts that accompany the work, such as large print, that is central to Jennifer's work being adopted in these galleries. These shows are gaining traction and shifts are taking place. Maria Balshaw, director of Tate Museum and Galleries, attended her latest show *To all the Kings that have no Crown* at the Carl Freedmam Gallery and more exhibitions planned for the future.

  * Blue chip refers to art galleries that show and sell art that is reliably profitable and expected to hold or increase its economic value.

International

The UK is significantly less progressive in comparison to other countries in terms of their practices in showing and valuing art from artists who don't follow the orthodox routes of art school and who identify as D/deaf, disabled, and neurodivergent. The USA has a number of galleries that work in this space and they aren't considered different and don't sit outside of the mainstream. The comparison is also stark in the way that these shows are portrayed in the press. Notable American art critics such as Jerry Saltz cover these shows in an engaged and respectful manner. This hasn't been the case in the UK. Jennifer has found that the coverage can actively 'other' the artists, framing their work in a deficit model and seeing their work as different and less. Jennifer is very careful how the work is portrayed so has grown wary and vigilant of the media, as this is where some of the largest perceptual barriers exist.

SHIFT

At the present time, the National Disability Arts Collection and Archive (NDACA), which documents the heritage story of the disability arts movement, does not have any representation of learning-disabled artists. This has led to Jennifer developing the initiative called SHIFT:

> SHIFT is about learning disabled and neurodivergent artists taking their rightful place around the table – having frank discussions, sharing ideas and articulating aims. It involves a shifting of focus, platforming and attitudes.

Change making on a national scale

Jennifer is also engaging national galleries such as Tate and The Baltic in a conversation around representation of the artists that she works with and is posing the question, what are the barriers to their inclusion in programming and how can they be overcome? She is facilitating these conversations alongside neurodivergent and disabled artists.

Graeae Theatre Company

Image 6.3 Graeae Theatre logo

As stated by Ruth Mackenzie, director of the London 2012 Cultural Olympiad, Graeae Theatre is 'a world-class theatre company that is artistically led by disabled people, pioneering an inclusive new dramatic language that is unparalleled and unprecedented'. She further comments that its reputation in this space is unparalleled: 'Graeae rightly holds iconic status nationally and internationally for the innovation and quality of its work. It plays a vital part in the cultural life of this country'.

Graeae Theatre Company was founded in 1980 by Nabil Shaban and Richard Tomlinson and, like both Action-Space and Drake Music, the majority of their funding comes from the Arts Council. The name of the company references the Graeae sisters of Greek legend and their belief in working collectively and sharing resources. Graeae clearly articulates its work in creating and exploring new spaces and across a range of genres with inclusion centrally located in its work.

Graeae champions the inclusion of deaf and disabled people in the arts through:

- Developing a new theatrical language in outdoor performance
- Investment in and nurturing Deaf and disabled artists
- Forging new collaborations and exchanges of skills with other companies

Inclusion and creativity

> *Access is a basic right and requirement, a continually evolving methodology that enhances the theatrical and professional landscape.*
>
> (Taken from Graeae's website)

Graeae's work in this space is the promotion of both access and representation. There is an overt commitment to, and ownership of, its inclusive practices that defines its identity and its creative output. It has an outward-looking perspective and views collective working and storytelling as a way of showing how inclusion is both a fundamental right but also a place of creative exploration.

Young people; growing the next generation of Deaf and disabled workshop leaders

> *Created in response to inaccessible mainstream drama training and a lack of diversity in the current theatre climate.*
>
> (Taken from Graeae's website)

A universal entitlement to engage in arts, as both producers and consumers, informs a rich programme of outreach and workshops in collaboration with partners. Graeae works across the educational landscape and through its programming has reached and worked with a large number of young people.

Interview with Jodi-Alissa Bickerton, creative learning director of Graeae Theatre

> *Our mantra at the moment is:* Nothing about us without us and we shall not be removed.

On access

> *What we try and do is cultivate an environment of support where everyone's access requirements are covered, and we are starting with the art, it's about the creativity.*

The personal and the political

> *We're blending the personal and the political; of course, those politics and those identities are going to become part of the characters that we are playing, or the DNA of a programme that we're running. Ultimately what we're trying to do is create a level playing field for a diversity of disabled artists.*

Activism

> *It's come from activism; it's come from the fact that we have been side-lined.*

We shall not be removed; the seven inclusive principles of an inclusive recovery

> *All these years, we continue to be side-lined, now that there's this reopening, we have been involved in a new disability movement which is one of the biggest memberships that disability movements ever had in the UK. It's called 'we shall not be removed' and there's some key people who have developed the seven inclusive principles of inclusive recovery; it's all about teaching organisations, cultural organisations, venues, schools, anyone. If you're reopening, don't forget about us.*

★ There is a link to the Graeae website that hosts 'the seven principles of an inclusive recovery' at the end of the chapter.

Innovation as a response to the pandemic

> *There's been a lot of positivity for us as an organisation because we will now never do another performance where there isn't digital streaming, all our performances will now be streamed, and the main character may indeed be in their lounge room.*

Young disabled voices

> *Without young people involved in those conversations (about the future) because they're the future that we're talking about, shaping arts and culture for a new world. We're going to be able to do that much better if we involve a more diverse community.*

The importance of the social model of disability

> *The social model of disability underpins part of our identity of being disabled, so we are saying that we are disabled, not by our impairment, but by our environment, and by misperceptions and attitudes.*

The issues of labels imposed; Special?

> *The charity model of disability; you are over there and you're a part of the excluded group and you are special. Young people don't call themselves special needs and if they do, it's because adults have told them that, so I just want young people to be involved in that, that change of term.*

Corali Dance Company

Image 6.4 Corali dance company logo

Corali Dance Company was founded in 1989 by social worker Virginia Moffat in Southwark, and in 1991 it received its first grant from the arts council of England. Like Graeae, ActionSpace, and Drake, it is a national portfolio organisation. Corali Dance Company is a disability-focused organisation, and Sarah Archdeacon is currently the artistic director.

Corali is a contemporary dance company that explores relationships with other art forms and between performers with and without learning disabilities. The company works with a range of stimuli to consider dance and performance in new ways, working across a variety of settings and in partnership with a range of cultural institutions such as Tate, the British Museum, and Sadler's Wells.

This progressive approach allows exploration and ownership for their artistic responses and creates space for creative connections to be made.

Performance and engagement

> Our dancers are at the heart of all our artistic activity, and our authenticity comes from their understanding of the world, unique creativity and talent.

> (Taken from Corali's website)

Corali develops and produces its own dance performances. They place collaboration and inclusion at the centre of their work. They also have a youth company called **Kick Up** that supports the development of their younger dancers. Through a programme of regular classes, workshops, residencies, and partnerships, there is a clear focus on collaboration and a genuine sense of ownership. Workshops are co-led with disabled and nondisabled facilitators; this unique relationship is one that I have witnessed and is elaborated on further in the interview with DJ.

Skills and carer development

Corali offers a programme to support carer development, this is supported by:

- A weekly professional development class led by skilled in-house artists alongside invited guest tutors
- Regular 1:1 mentoring to identify individual development goals and further opportunities
- Skills exchange with other professional artists with and without learning disabilities
- LAB – intensive workshops for dancers to research and develop their ideas
- Kick Up –developing future generations of dance artists through their youth company
- Are You Ready? – an accredited programme for young dancers run every other year

Role models and activism

Everyone has a story to tell – a conversation with DJ, associate artistic director at Corali Dance Company

The following writing is based on a conversation that DJ had with Paul Morrow and Sarah Archdeacon.

Our conversations moved across a number of topics and demonstrated how passionate DJ is as a dancer, a teacher, and the associate artistic director of Corali.

For DJ, dancing is a profound art, one where changes take place. 'Everyone has stories to tell'. DJ describes the power of dancing and how for him it enables him to tell stories and make connections. DJ speaks very poetically about how dancing makes him feel, describing how it allows him to become a 'free spirit' but also how he uses dance to interact. 'I give my voice, my heart, who I am, I connect'.

Hidden away

'Hidden away' is the way that DJ describes how some people who have disabilities feel – 'hidden away from their bodies'. DJ talks about how at Corali everyone is valued and that through dance a transformation takes place. DJ comments, 'I see a difference in them, everyone is somebody, and everyone's got a life'. The importance of dancing and how this can release people is clear. For DJ the act of dancing is liberating, and everyone has the 'right to be happy and right to be who they are'.

At Corali DJ works alongside Sarah and they have between themselves developed a way of facilitating dance where their partnership has grown into a very inclusive model of dance. There is real rapport between DJ and Sarah, and this is evident in the way he talks about how they work together. DJ describes their partnership as one that is 'ground breaking' and where they 'feed off each other' and that they are a 'unit'. Sarah described how generous DJ was with his skills, and ability to give.

DJ is a role model, but mindful of what the term means. He discusses his practice as a journey with a sense of purpose. DJ and Sarah spent time clarifying what a role model was. For DJ 'it's a complex thing' and 'it's about confidence'. He talks about how he is 'proud and confident' and that authenticity is key. It's 'not about pretending', and he takes it very seriously as it is 'power with responsibility'.

DJ is an activist. His teaching and performance are creative, but there is a moral purpose to his work; 'I would like to change people, respect and understand each other, connect people'. Dance and its ability to connect people is made clear by DJ. That through his dance and his teaching DJ makes a 'creative space for change'.

One thing is clear – DJ is on a mission with his work at Corali where he says that he has a 'passion to make a difference'. I'm sure that this is happening and will continue to happen, as in his own words DJ is a 'tough cookie and I won't crumble'.

* First published as a blog for the Cultural Inclusion Manifesto.

Summary of key points

- All adopted the social model of inclusion
- All adopted structural approaches to inclusion within their organisation
- All organisations had a dual purpose of activism and creativity
- Partnership working is central to their mission to promote inclusion and creative practice
- Creating opportunities for employment and routes to work were also part of their practice
- The creative artistic opportunities that inclusion can create, and innovation was central to practice

---

The inclusive canon: a vehicle for change

The concept for the inclusive canon was developed for a number of reasons. The first was the lack of representation of D/deaf, disabled, and neurodivergent artists, musicians, and dancers in general. The second was the increased focus on cultural capital within the Ofsted framework and, as mentioned earlier in the book, the SEND code of practice. The latter states:

> It can be particularly powerful to meet disabled adults who are successful in their work, or who have made significant contribution to their community' and 'High aspirations about employment, independent living and community participation should be developed through the curriculum and extra-curriculum provision. (SEN Code of Practice, 2015:124).

The importance of cultural capital, and the need for schools to articulate it, presents an opportunity to address this imbalance.

Nnena Kalu

Nnena Kalu is one such artist whose practice merits being celebrated and included within the inclusive canon. Nnena has developed her artistic practice at ActionSpace's studio in Studio Voltaire since 1999 where her work has gained much acclaim. Nnena has exhibited nationally and internationally, building a significant body of work over 20 years and is currently one of 20 visual artists to receive the Paul Hamlyn Foundations Artist Award. Nnena's first major London-based solo commission for 'elsewhere', Studio Voltaire's offsite programme in 2020.

Using disability-led and disability-focused organisations to support the Gatsby benchmark number 5 and positive career outcomes

Gatsby benchmark 5; encounters with employers and employees

We have touched on the idea of role models with the interview with DJ and his role as an associate artistic director at Corali and the idea of the inclusive canon. However, a more strategic approach can embed these organisations further and help young people's transition into employment.

All these organisations have identified the need to create pathways for young people, and working strategically with schools can be a mutually beneficial way of achieving this. There is enormous value in developing relationships with disability-led/disability-focused organisations to ensure that employers and employees represent diverse bodies and minds in a meaningful, appropriate, and engaging manner.

What good looks like

Every student should have multiple opportunities to learn from employers about work, employment, and the skills that are valued in the workplace. This can be through a range of enrichment activities, including visiting speakers, mentoring, and enterprise schemes.

- All young people in years 7–13 should have at least one encounter a year by 2020, in line with the Gatsby benchmarks.
- Meaningful encounters cover a range of activities with employers, both in and outside the school, but does not include off-site experiences of workplaces.

(Taken from The SEND Gatsby Benchmark Toolkit, Practical information and guidance for schools, special schools and colleges, Second Edition)

This is supported by research that describes a number of 'encounters' for the impact to be effective. This also chimes with the notion of a culture of high expectations and a person-centred approach as set out in the SEND code of practice (2015).

Practical ideas that can support this

Arts Award: using disability-led and disability-focused organisations in inclusive arts qualifications

Arts Award is an art qualification that is structurally inclusive. Unlike GCSE or Entry Level, it isn't time bound and it offers a framework that can support enquiry and help to develop meaningful partnerships with arts organisations. The way in which you can collect evidence is also inclusive. Evidence can be from a variety of formats and can be collected in lots of creative ways, from workbooks and sketch books to videos, photographs, and teacher annotations, as long as it corresponds to and meets the criteria and demonstrates the learning journey of the student.

There are opportunities to embed these organisations meaningfully within these qualifications

Arts Award Discover
Part B; Find out
What young people should do:

Young people find out about **at least one artist** and their work to develop understanding of arts practice. This could be through workshops, interviews, online interactions, visits, attending events, research, or other methods. They should be **supported to develop responses to what they find out**.

Arts Award Explore

Part B; Explore

What young people should do:

Young people explore the work of **at least one artist** and **one arts organisation through live or active experience**. The artist and arts organisation can be local, national, or international and of any size and scale.
  Arts organisations can include museums, libraries, or other organisations or companies that support work in the arts. Young people should focus on arts-related work of the organisation and the people involved in this work. Artists and arts organisations may be connected through art form or location, or they may be entirely different.

Lots of cultural organisations can support with the delivery of arts award

Most national portfolio organisations (NPOs) funded by Arts Council will be familiar with the qualifications and be able to offer support in achieving the award. More information can be found at the Arts Award website at the end of the chapter.

Themed weeks

These are great opportunities to explore these organisations in more depth and to run workshops and celebration events to develop meaningful relationships with disability-focused/disability-led organisations.

Careers week

During careers week, or within your schools, you can profile these organisations and promote them, so that these organisations, their programming, and their pathways are made visible to the young people you work with.

Concluding notes

This chapter explores the principle of inclusion by looking at disabled-led and disabled-focused organisations. The chapter demonstrates the importance of making connections with organisations so that disabled students can see a trajectory within this space, that they can be actors, artists, dancers, and musicians. The chapter makes the case for increasing the range of artists and art organisations that schools engage with so that they are truly inclusive and representative of the wider society. Nnena Kalu is mentioned in this chapter as an artist who should be used within the inclusive canon. Her practice is further unpacked in chapter 9, exploring how contemporary art and artists can support inclusive pedagogy.

Reference

Special educational needs and disability code of practice: 0 to 25 years Statutory guidance for organisations which work with and support children and young people who have special educational needs or disabilities January 2015.

Useful websites

Drake Music

www.drakemusic.org

ActionSpace

www.actionspace.org

Graeae

www.graeae.org

Corali dance

www.corali.org.uk

European outsider art association

www.outsiderartassociation.eu

Disability arts online

Online directory of disability-focused and disability-led organisations:
www.disabilityarts.online

#weshallnotberemoved

www.weshallnotberemoved.com
This website contains information on the seven inclusive principles to ensure an inclusive recovery.

Unlimited

www.weareunlimited.org.uk

National Disability Arts Collection and Archive

www.the-ndaca.org

Arts Award

www.artsaward.org.uk

---

7 Cultural inclusion – a historical perspective

Participation and representation over the years

It is important to view cultural inclusion within a historical context. All cultural production is essentially storytelling, and the narratives shared help to shape perceptions of disabled people and impact significantly on their own sense of self and the worth and value that society places on them.

This chapter explores some of these narratives around disabled people and how they have helped to form views and perceptions of people with disabilities. Historically there have been instances where people with disabilities have been portrayed, and they have led to the formation of stereotypes. This chapter will unpack some of these, so that they can be made visible and challenged, for as Prince describes, 'The cost of negative beliefs or inaccurate information is high, both for people with disabilities and for society as a whole' (Prince, 2006:20).

How to use this chapter

This chapter will inform you of the power of representation and helps to shine a light on the portrayal of disabilities and how this has formed societal views. The focus here is to make these real, for you the reader to be aware of these constructs and how they can affect you as the consumer of culture. Once these stereotypes are revealed, there is an ethical case to challenge them whenever they present, and this further establishes the argument for an anti-ableist pedagogy that reframes disability as a positive and promotes inclusion for all. Anti-ableist pedagogy is a fundamental strand of inclusion. Chapter 8 looks at how this can be practically supported through teaching practices and assessment using a case study that gives specific examples.

The power of representation

The representation of disabled people within arts and culture has the power to influence the wider societal view. In the words of Barnes this can be 'fundamental to the discrimination and exploitation which disabled people encounter daily and contribute significantly to their systematic exclusion from mainstream community life' (Barnes, 1992:39). Barnes was referring to the portrayal of disabilities within literature, but the portrayal of disabilities across all art forms has implications. Barnes powerfully describes these implications and their direct effects on people's lives.

A historical framework

It is important to frame the conversation of cultural inclusion within a historical context and to acknowledge that this is a power dynamic that still exists today. This is explored later in the chapter in an interview with Dr Claire Penketh of Liverpool Hope University.

Childhood and the shaping of perceptions

Nursery rhymes are a common occurrence in all our childhoods, and it is here that we first encounter exclusionary material. *Simple Simon* is a historical nursery rhyme from the seventeenth century that describes a young boy who makes several mishaps. The origin of the rhyme has many variations. However, the word Simple Simon has led to the word describing someone who is a *fool* or a *gullible person*. Another example is that of *Three Blind Mice*, a nursey rhyme associated with three Protestant lords tortured at the hands of the devout Catholic Mary Stuart (Bloody Mary) and her husband King Phillippe of Spain. The rhyme demonstrates historical attitudes towards disabilities with the song's casual mockery of the mice's visual impairment. From childhood we are exposed to an all-pervasive diet of representation where identities in relation to disabilities are formed and which lead to stereotypes.

DOI: 10.4324/9781003122258-7

Stereotypes and metaphors

The role that cultural production has in forming and constructing societal views of disabilities is profound. It is through this lens that people develop opinions, views, and concepts of disabilities and where cultural values are formed. The historical depiction of disabilities has led to associated identities and characteristics. These constructs have led to the formation of stereotypes, stereotypes that have a corresponding notion of 'values' attached to these characteristics. These stereotypes are limiting and often negative in nature, placing people with disabilities within a deficit model. This portrayal has led to and enforced a societal view of disabilities. The notion of stereotypes and the attribution of a set of characteristics align with the previous chapter's discussion on *labelling* and the notion of 'othering'. These stereotypes tend to fall into three distinct categories: victim, hero, and villain.

Stereotype: the victim

One depiction of this can be seen within Charles Dickens's portrayal of Tiny Tim. Not much is known of Tim's character; he is defined by his disability, a character whose disability becomes a device that is used to garner sympathy from the audience. His disability is used as both a means of condemning Ebenezer Scrooge and the source of his redemption. The use of this device places and portrays the character of Tiny Tim as the victim, an object of pity and sympathy known only through his disability.

Stereotype: the hero

This refers to the portrayal of disabled people as heroes, where their worth is derived from their ability to overcome their disability to conform to a notion of normalcy. The hero stereotype has been described as the 'supercrip'. This term describes when a disabled person achieves something 'heroic' and through this process has become more 'normal'. An example of this can be seen in the film *My Left Foot* by the Irish writer Christy Brown, who described it as 'plucky little cripple story'. The hero stereotype focuses on an individual, framing them as someone who has succeeded despite of their disability and then uses this as a benchmark against all those that live with their disability. It frames disability as something to be overcome, supports the concept of normalcy, and places the labour of accommodating the disabled person back on them as they need to 'try harder' to 'fit in'.

Stereotype: the villain

One such example of this stereotype is that found in pirate stories. Many of these stories were written a long time ago and demonstrate how these stereotypes were historically formed. The stereotype can be found in how these characters are described – their physical disability is an outward sign of their villainy. It can be seen in those characters that have lost an eye, or a leg; one such example of this is Captain Hook in Peter Pan. This stereotype can also be seen within Shakespearian plays and his portrayal of Richard III. Richard III is often used as an example of this stereotype due in part to the fame of Shakespeare within the canon of English literature and how pervasive these stereotypes are. In the play *Richard III*, Richard describes himself as an 'ugly hunchback', and he is portrayed as evil, scheming, jealous, and murderous.

Additional stereotypes

The savant

Savant originates from the French word *savoir* meaning 'to know'. This stereotype can be seen as similar to the notion of the savant, most commonly associated with autistic spectrum condition (ASC). The construct of the savant is located within the deficit model. The disabled person's 'gift' or talent is juxtaposed with their disability, and this adds to this notion of superhuman ability. This is clearly seen within Darold A. Treffert's abstract for his synopsis: *The savant syndrome: an extraordinary condition. A synopsis: past, present, future*, where he describes the autistic savant as 'a rare, but extraordinary, condition in which persons with serious mental disabilities, including autistic disorder, have some '"island of genius" which stands in marked, incongruous contrast to overall handicap.'

This description clearly situates this within a deficit model. It demonstrates how this stereotype further adds to a wider societal view, a view that enforces ideas of ableism and sits is in stark contrast to the social model of inclusion.

The eternal child

This trope is often found in literature and frames disability and particularly that of cognitive disability within a childhood timeframe. It positions disabled characteristics as childlike and with no opportunity to develop, grow, and transition into adulthood. It is a trope that denies the disabled character the full human experience and the transitions that take place over time. It creates tensions particularly around sex and sexuality. It also acts as a barrier to the development of identity, agency, and personhood.

Contemporary stereotypes: The Joker

The use of negative stereotypes can also be seen within the contemporary film *The Joker* and its use of mental health as a device to account for his behaviour. The presentation of his declining mental health in the film and its correspondence with increased violence towards others is used as a plot device and further embeds the villainous stereotype into society. It is commonly known that people who have mental illness are more likely to experience violence than to be the perpetrator of violence.

The fundamental issue with stereotypes is that they dehumanise

Stereotypes at their worse use disability as an outward symbol of negative characteristics and at the opposite end of the spectrum offer an unrealistic, inauthentic projection of a person based primarily on their disability. Stereotypes deny people their personhood and their right to be seen and acknowledged as an individual.

Task: How storytelling shape's societal view, discuss

It can be helpful to reflect these devices back at students so that they can become conscious of stereotypes and challenge them.

- You might consider presenting a part of the text and ask students to comment on this, to consider it through the framework of these stereotypes and ask them to comment. You might ask them to consider when they have encountered a stereotype and to consider how it might affect how people are perceived
- You could juxtapose this text with a contemporary inclusive piece of writing and ask students to comment. After introducing them to the concept of stereotypes, you could introduce them to the concept of personhood

Personhood

Personhood is the right to have rights. Personhood is to be acknowledged and seen as an equal with human value and dignity.

Other practical ways to be more inclusive in your classroom

Make sure that your learning resources are inclusive of disabled people. If you use PowerPoint slides and there are characters in them, make sure that they are inclusive and that disabled characters are included. Audit your learning environment and make sure that star charts/displays are inclusive and include images of disabled students. These things don't take long, but the messaging in them can be very powerful.

Invisibility: seen but not acknowledged

The portrayal and use of people with disabilities as a metaphor within film, drama, and literature has been widely acknowledged. Metaphors use a concrete image to communicate something abstract and are reliant on the assumption of a universal understanding of what the metaphor represents.

These metaphors can refer to a wider social issue or comment on personality or character as demonstrated earlier with Tiny Tim and Richard III. A contemporary example of this can be seen with the depiction of supervillains within James Bond films; these supervillains usually have some overt visual disability that is used as a metaphor. This device can also be seen within the Star Wars series of films where the facial disfigurement of Darth Vader is an outward metaphor of his malignant intent. Disabled people have also been used as a plot device for their able-bodied, neurotypical counterparts, presented as two-dimensional characters whose disability is their defining characteristic. Here the notion of invisibility is ubiquitous – always there, yet in the background and not acknowledged. Snyder et al. (2002) describe this use of disability within the field of literature as ever present, seen, yet not acknowledged and consistently perpetuating a condition of otherness.

Often encountered, rarely acknowledged

Through researching these constructs of disabled identities, it surprised me how often we encounter these stereotypes, unaware of them as they are so deeply embedded. It's only through being mindful of these constructs that they are revealed and can be questioned, scrutinised, and challenged.

Of Mice and Men: far-reaching implications for the representation of disability

I chose to explore this representation of disability as it was one that I had encountered, like many others have, during my time at school studying English, and it is seen very much as part of the literary canon of both the UK and the USA. The book was part of the GCSE examination syllabus until 2014 when it was removed to focus on British writers. The book still remains popular and is often used in key stage three.

The book also offers some insight through its narrative of how disabilities were conceptualised at the time of its writing. The characteristics attributed to Lennie's character fall into those broad categories of stereotypes as described earlier in the chapter.

A modern classic

The book is widely seen as a modern classic, however when examined through the lens of inclusion the use of stereotypes is problematic. The character of Lennie has learning difficulties and a cognitive disability, and he also demonstrates some autistic character traits: repetitive behaviours, echolalia (repeating of words), and sensory-seeking behaviours, such as wanting to touch the soft fur of the animals. Interestingly the book was written before the condition was identified in 1943 by Leo Kanner. The book also illustrates the far-reaching impacts of the cultural reproduction of stereotypes, the power that they have, and their direct impact on societal systems and, in this case, the legal system. The book was written by John Steinbeck in 1937 around the same time as the eugenics movement was gaining traction in the United States. This historical context and the ultimate ending of the book also have significance in relation to the 'Briseño' factor.

'Briseño' factor

This is a legal device used in the state of Texas to decide on a prisoner's suitability to face the death penalty and was written by the Texas Court of Criminal Appeals. It asks the citizens of Texas to compare the inmate on trial to the character of Lennie and states, (Taken from Judge Cochran's 2004 opinion that became de facto law).

The implications of this are extraordinary. It implies that an individual that seems less cognitively disabled than Lenny would not be exempt. The Briseño factors are not recognised by a single clinical or scientific body. They are based on a literary construct of disabilities from the 1930s. The state of Texas at the time of writing still uses the phrase 'mental retardation'.

Lennie the eternal child

Lennie's character is portrayed like that of a child. His interest in animals is framed with childlike enthusiasm, and his repeated requests for George to repeat the story of how they would live off the land is similar to a child requesting a story from a 'grown up'. Lennie's sexuality is also a point of tension. George excludes Lennie from visiting the 'cat house', giving the impression that for Lennie to be sexually active would be wrong. Lennie is reliant on George throughout the narrative; George denies Lennie his sexuality and agency and consequently his personhood. George is given the parental role within the relationship, but also a role where he can be judge, jury, and executioner. Lennie could also be seen as a plot device for George, the story based on how George responds to Lennie and his relationship with Lennie. George is positioned as the superior within a relationship of unequals.

Stereotype villain

Lennie's cognitive disability and his violent acts are portrayed as his defining characteristics; his 'otherness' is highlighted in relation to other characters, as is his reliance on George.

He is portrayed here in several ways that chimes with stereotypes; he is a monstrous, and he is also used a plot device for George and ultimately the decision that George takes at the end of the book.

Books that portray disability positively

The following is just some of books that you could use to portray disability positively. There are a lot more out there. Using these books can also show how your school is supporting its duty to promote equality of opportunity, awareness, and understanding of rights under the Equality Act.

Books that promote positive portrayals of disability

- *Seal Surfer*, by Michael Foreman (reading ages 6+)
- *Harriet Versus the Galaxy*, by Samantha Baines (reading age 7+)
- *Cally and Jimmy: Twins in Trouble*, by Zoe Antoniades (reading age 7+)
- *Song for a Whale*, by Pippa Goodhart (reading age 9+)
- *A Dog Called Flow*, by Pippa Goodhart (reading age 7+)
- *The Boy with the Butterfly Mind*, by Victoria Williamson (reading age 9+)
- *The Amazing Edie Eckhart Book 1*, by Rosie Jones (reading age 9+)
- *Scarlet Ibis*, by Gill Lewis, by (reading ages 9+)
- *Future Girl*, by Asphyxia (reading ages 13+)
- *Rosie Loves Jack*, by Mel Darbon (reading ages 13+)

Hidden histories: the culture of disabled arts and crafts within institutions

A conversation with Dr Claire Penketh, subject lead for Disability Studies at Liverpool Hope University.

The conversation is punctuated by questions and provocations that you could reflect on professionally, or they could be used as a stimulus for discussions with students and colleagues.

Questions

The questions were designed as prompts to support the conversation; the questions were:

Identity and cultural value

From the perspective of disability studies and in relation to the making of art and craft and the perceived societal value, how have the historic identities (stereotypes) affected their perceived value?

Hidden histories

How has this impacted on disabled people's exclusion from cultural spaces?

Identity and cultural value: the hidden histories of institutions

The conversation

The conversation with Dr Penketh explored disability arts and crafts through a historical lens and the educational discourses that have informed disabled identities.

A significant historical strand of the relationship between disability arts and arts education is located within institutions of segregation and linked to the history of exclusion. These histories are there, however they exist in a historical space of separateness, as Dr Penketh asserts:

> There are histories of disability, but because of the way that society has evolved, you have to look in different places for those histories. And so, we look at the histories of institutions.

Institutional histories and the cultural spaces inhabited by arts and crafts made by disabled people

Dr Penketh gives the example:

> If you look into the history of the Royal School for the Blind in Liverpool, my argument is you will find histories of a relationship between disability and art, craft and design education within those histories. 'However, these

histories aren't documented: 'They're not drawn out and made explicit and I think there's something interesting that happens there. The way that that disability is treated, but also the way that arts education is treated within those institutions.

> **Questions/provocation**
>
> • Could you look for hidden histories within your cultural partners? Stories that aren't told and give them focus? It could be in an art lesson, it could be through an issues-based piece of work
> • You could look within your own institution and see how history and imagery are used
> • Cultural partners could look at exploring their own institution or alongside a school, giving a platform for new and different narratives to be explored and different perspectives to be presented

A culture of crafting

With the emergence of such institutions a culture of crafting developed, and within these institutions the educational structures that would support this.

This cultural production wasn't seen or valued in the way that mainstream cultural production was valued at the time. The products made were seen as a means of survival – the crafts produced would in part fund the institution and be a way of attracting more benefactors. These institutions developed crafting classes so that the products could be sold, but through these activities they were also developing an educational culture, as Dr Penketh explains:

> People who may not have had employment were engaged in craft workshops, and the argument could be actually that those craft workshops are some of the first forms of inclusion and emphasis on people being able to learn skills, so that they could eventually be employed.

And:

> It was part of sustaining the institution, it took people three years to be able to learn the skills of things like basket weaving. I just thought, three years working on a regular basis, so this idea that it took three years to develop these skills, that's an apprenticeship.

> **Questions/provocation**
>
> • Consider how value is constructed in art, craft, and design, where the work is made and where the work is viewed can affect this. Consider how you make judgements and ask the students to describe what imagery or artefacts they give value to and why that is.
> • Introduce students to this concept so that they can be aware of these judgements, show them work displayed in a gallery, graffiti, and work made in a crafting class and ask them to think about which has the most cultural value and which has the least value, and why that is.

An emerging pedagogy

Within these spaces of segregation a culture of learning was emerging and alongside it the first instances of exhibition. However, the display of work was very much within that space of difference.

Dr Penketh explains this as 'The exclusion from cultural spaces, and in essence the motivation to show their work was to increase their income into those institutions'.

Contemporary interpretations of historical practices

Looking from a contemporary viewpoint to evaluate and critique practices that started in the nineteenth century is problematic. There needs to be a historical contextual understanding when looking at these institutions. As Dr Penketh explains, 'Reading those histories of the institutions and look to how those practices are occurring'. These institutions of separateness were also a place where a culture of disabled arts and crafts was emerging; they inhabit a complex space of contradictions. Penketh cites the work of French academic Henri-Jacques Striker, who acknowledges that these institutions were places of separation; however, it is also in these institutions that practices of inclusion start to emerge. The tension is that they in themselves also developed disabling practices.

Institutional histories: unequal voices

The histories that were told, recorded, and celebrated were typically from those of the benefactor, as Dr Penketh describes. 'The Perkins schools established by sighted benefactors on behalf of blind people, so the actual contribution that disabled people make is sometimes missing'. The Perkins School for the Blind in the USA was founded in 1829 and has notable alumni, including Helen Keller. Penketh gives an example of this: 'One of the teachers was a blind person and was a teacher, and then there's very little information about that person. You can't find it. But to me, that's really compelling. This was somebody with visual impairment who had pedagogic skills, who was teaching other people who are blind'.

Art, craft, and design pedagogy and the construction of disabled identities

'I would argue that critical explorations of disability are still less evident in Art Education'. This quote from Dr Penketh enforces the idea that histories of art education are exclusionary. Dr Penketh describes that they 'Assume a particular norm, so, disability isn't explicitly or is rarely mentioned'. The historical examination of art and design education excludes disabilities, and the legacy of this still permeates the structures and narratives that inform education more generally today. Educational discourses of art and design are informed by those that are at play in wider society. These discourses directly inform the way in which art and design has been conceptualised and how teaching was enacted, and they have directly impacted on how disabled identities have been formed. From the industrial revolution of the eighteenth century and the idea of draughtsmanship to the need for skills and dexterity and for technically accurate design to service the economy, there have been a range of discourses that have informed disabled identities.

Alongside this economic driver within education, a modern concept of disabilities also emerges and gives rise to the idea of what Penketh explains as the 'Productive and non-productive bodies'. This focus on technical ability within art education promoted a skills-based pedagogy. Another contributing narrative was, and still is, the idea of the 'child' and the concept of child development that correspond with this. This development started to, and still does, inform ideas within art and design teaching that mirrors this model of development. The formation of these historical discourses started to frame disability, from those that describe skills to those that promote the ideals of beauty, expression, and the high art of Romanticism. These discourses also framed the identities of those who didn't conform to these ideals as something outside, as separate from and not part of these discourses.

Concluding notes

This pivotal chapter contextualises how disability has been framed historically and how this has informed how we teach and the educational structures that frame disability. This chapter makes the case for change and how we, as educationalists, have the duty to tell histories that include and are inclusive.

The following chapter, chapter 8, examines anti-ableist pedagogy. The importance of understanding this pedagogy is central so that we can, as the DFE teaching standard number five states, 'Adapt teaching to respond to the strengths and needs of all pupils'.

Bibliography/further reading

Barnes, C. (1992) *Disabling Imagery and the Media: An Exploration of the Principles for Media Representations of Disabled People*. Halifax: BCOPD/Ryburn Publishing.

Loftis, S.F. (2016) The autistic victim: Of mice and men. In Davis, L.J. (ed.), *Disability Studies Reader*, pp. 470–480, 5th edn. New York: Routledge.

Prince, M.J. (2006) *Pride and Prejudice: The Ambivalence of Canadian Attitudes toward Disability and Inclusion*. Toronto: L'Institut Roeher Institute.

Snyder, S.L., Brueggemann, B.J. and Thomson, R.G. (2002) *Disability Studies: Enabling the Humanities*. New York: Modern Language Association of America.

Journal

Treffert, D.A. (June, 2009) The savant syndrome: An extraordinary condition: A synopsis: Past, present, future. Philosophical Transactions B of the Royal Society 364, 1351–1357.

8 Anti-ableist pedagogy in arts and culture

In this chapter we will explore ableism and define what anti-ableist pedagogy is in arts and culture and how it can be practically supported in the classroom.

We will explore this through case studies that draw out the characteristics of anti-ableist pedagogy and give practical guidance on how it can be replicated. The case study approach draws out these characteristics in the hope that they can then be amplified or scaled up to be guiding principles for practice and employed in a number of settings. This chapter will also draw out some of the theory that underpins this approach to support your understanding of the wider implications.

Anti-ableism, inclusion, and critical pedagogy

I am very lucky to be involved in a National Society for Education in Art and Design (NSEAD) special interest group for advancing anti-ableist pedagogy, and this has directly informed some of the work within this chapter. I would like to thank them for drawing my attention to the importance of establishing this discourse within art and design education and wider pedagogy.

This chapter also chimes with the inclusive pedagogy described in Chapter 9, which explores contemporary art practice and pedagogy. The inclusive pedagogy described in the chapter can also be described as anti-ableist, as both inclusion and anti-ableist pedagogies are closely aligned.

Anti-ableist pedagogy corresponds with the work of the influential thinkers of critical pedagogy such as bell hooks and Paulo Freire, both of whom saw education as a place and space for positive change for individuals and groups. Critical pedagogy questions practices that are repressive; it is the pedagogy that is transformational through its practices. These principles correspond to the social model of inclusion in that they both promote positive change.

Anti-ableism and disablism

The two words are similar in that they both describe discrimination and prejudice towards disabled people. However, there are differences. Disablism describes direct and overt discrimination and prejudice. Ableism describes discriminatory behaviours that favour nondisabled people.

This chapter also refers to the chapter on policy and strategy that explores protected characteristics within education policy, with disability being one of these characteristics where not only are anti-ableist pedagogies essential but also should be actively promoted. It is schools' duty as a public body to 'actively advance equality of opportunity between people who share a protected characteristic and people who do not share it' and 'Foster good relations across all protected characteristics – between people who share a protected characteristic and people who do not share it' (taken from the Public Sector Equality Duty [the Equality Duty] which was created by the Equality Act 2010).

How to use this chapter

This chapter looks at how inclusive pedagogy and assessment can be embedded within a project and articulates this in relation to anti-ableist pedagogy. It considers how the project was planned, what the guiding principles were, how the project was delivered and assessed, and what the characteristics were of this practice that located it as anti-ableist. This information is also distilled into one table at the end of the chapter. Throughout the chapter, **Top tips** are used to draw out characteristics that can support the development delivery and assessment of work or a project and can help in developing an anti-ableist approach.

What do we mean by anti-ableism pedagogy?

As mentioned in earlier chapters the concept of ableism refers to the idea that the world, its structures, and the way that it is organised through these structures, both physical and societal, are developed in relation to normalcy and the

DOI: 10.4324/9781003122258-8

able–bodied that was explored in detail in the introductory chapter. These attitudes and structures devalue and place limitations on those who do not conform. Ableism is discrimination and/or prejudice that may be intentional or unintentional. These prejudices can be seen within culture and education in terms of representation, participation, and access. See also chapter 12, titled 'Relaxed performances and venues', in which Jess Thom of Touretteshero discusses some of her experiences.

Ableism in education

This can take many forms. It is particularly overt when education is promoting through practice(s) and assessment the notion of normalcy.

For example, ableism can present in a scheme of work that is fixed within a linear sense of progression without capacity for lateral progression or enquiry. It has a premeditated idea of what success is with a fixed idea of what progress looks like. Fixed ideas mean that there are no mechanisms where teaching involves or is informed by the learner or is co-produced or co-constructed. There is a lack of opportunity-based learning, and the scheme of work is informed and contextualised by limiting cultural models and cultural references. It places the emphasis on the product rather than the process and is assessed against an externalised assessment criterion. Some of these have been distilled into the following table.

The descriptors mentioned earlier give a sense of how ableism might present within teaching practices. These are just general descriptors, and they might be encountered all together or separately. The one common factor is that they marginalise. These characteristics pathologise difference, promoting one singular way of accessing and achieving, and pathologise disabilities. So, what might the characteristics of anti-ableist pedagogy be?

The following descriptors describe those characteristics of anti-ableist pedagogy.

Anti-ableism in education

1. There is a broad and inclusive range of cultural references that are being promoted and used to contextualise learning, drawing on artists who are also D/deaf, disabled, and neurodivergent and from different ethnic and socioeconomic backgrounds
2. Planning supports learning and anticipates need but creates a framework to teach within that has flexibility and contingency and is inclusive of the learner, and opportunities for learning are built upon when presented
3. Process is valued and the journey of learning given status
4. The student is located centrally within the teaching
5. Differences in being, seeing, and experiencing are seen as assets and offer creative opportunities for enquiry
6. There are multiple entry points, and these are informed by the students
7. Learning is co-constructed, and the student is fully acknowledged and is central within this process
8. Assessment is qualitative in approach and tells the story of the student's learning using both ipsative and narrative assessment
9. Diversity of outcomes illustrate a structurally inclusive and anti-ableist approach

---

Case study: Open City architectural project

Context/background

This is the second year of the SEND Architects in Schools project. The aim of this project is for the students to engage with architecture, architects, and the built environment. The project was facilitated by an artist, a musician, an architect, and the organisation's facilitator and ran for several weeks.

★ I would like to acknowledge and thank Open City for allowing me to use their evaluation of the project that has directly informed this case study.

The case study looks at the following key points and extracts key characteristics that could be replicated within practice:

The case study describes:

- Context
- The project and the main protagonists
- Structure
- Evaluation and assessment approaches
- Diversity and difference as positives

- Planning the project
- Pedagogy
- Creativity and inclusive anti-ableist pedagogy
- Objectives first day and setting the scene
- Material curiosity
- Learning spaces
- Diversity of outcomes; an inclusive and anti-ableist signifier
- Impromptu displays/celebrations
- Wider implications

The protagonists

The artist and the musician

The artist and the musician contributed their skills and knowledge of creative practice. Marc the artist and Luke the musician had a long history of working together and intuitively, where they would present and entice the students to engage. There was a fluidity and improvisation that informed their approaches. Marc's understanding of artistic expression and enquiry with a specific interest in material exploration was complemented by Luke's musical approach. Luke looked at how the music could shape and inform learning, how it could support transitions into work and enhance the learning experience, interpreting and responding to them to facilitate a deeper enquiry.

The facilitator

Sarah Phillips, Head of Education and Empowerment at Open City, offered an educational viewpoint and mediated the conversations as the project manager, chairing and supporting the conversations, facilitating, and supporting the co-production of the project and capturing the learning journey.

The teacher and the class team

The teacher and the class team offered their knowledge of each of the learner's motivations and interests and advised on the structure of the day to ensure that this would also support the engagement and enjoyment of the students.

★ Students on the autism spectrum usually have specific interests that they find highly motivating and engaging, and it is an approach that the school uses with its students to support and facilitate their learning.

The students

The project was run with a group of primary students who were all diagnosed with an autistic spectrum condition. The project was to be delivered in the art room for six weeks where the students would access the space in small groups over the course of the day.

Lead practitioner (me)

I had the privilege of brokering and supporting the project. I was keen to ensure that there was equity within the partnership and that we all actively listened, learned, and adapted the project as a response to co-production and co-construction.

Structure

Shared common language

Shared common language is useful in conceptualising and supporting projects.

One word that was consistently used to describe interactions between the students and the facilitators and allowed for creative spaces to be shaped, explored, and realised was curious. Curious is a word that was helpful in illustrating this way of working and was used consistently across the project as it evolved.

Structurally embedded

It was made clear from the genesis of the project that an inclusive and anti-ableist approach would underpin the project. This was discussed and signposted to and it was embedded through regular conversations. Conversations were informal during the course of the session and allowed for change, adaptation, and response and for extending the learning. They were also used to consider the next steps in the student's journey of learning.

The method of assessing and evaluating the project was also inclusive and looked at each child's point of entry and the way in which the project developed to support them in their creative enquiry. This way of evaluating and assessing is ipsative, as discussed in chapter 9 exploring contemporary art, in that it articulates learning in relation to that specific learner and their entry point or baseline into the project.

Be curious: a journey of learning and co-construction

Getting to know you and *building rapport* were objectives of the project, and this supported the impact and the personalisation of the learning. The first session was designed as purely a getting to know you day, one where activities were planned based on the knowledge of the students the teacher had shared with the artists, but flexibility, improvisation, and finding out were given high status.

A journey of learning had begun . . .

Top tips

- Introduce everyone and be clear about roles
- Understand what co-production is, describe this and how you have structurally embedded it within the project/pedagogy
- Promote shared common language and understanding of the objectives
- Use an ipsative assessment model, pertinent and descriptive of the student's entry points to their learning
- Make time for evaluations; these can be informal conversations
- Name the way you have chosen to work – co-produced learning – and give it status
- Inclusive person-centric approaches are also anti-ableist

Diversity and difference as a positive

The teaching approaches used within the project located it within the social model of inclusion. Difference wasn't pathologised – it was seen as an asset and a positive and a space for creative exploration. The project made this position overt using the word curious as a means of describing this approach in how the teachers interacted and observed the students and their response. To be curious of the learner and interested also meant that they were seen, that they were acknowledged as an equitable partner within the learning relationship. The word curious was also used to frame how students interacted with activities and materials, and this approach gave space and named how the learning was co-produced.

Acknowledge the learner

Being authentically 'seen' and having your personhood acknowledged is essential to an anti-ableist pedagogy. This again refers to the idea of being curious, curious and interested in the student and in how and in what way they are engaging.

Tip tips

- Be curious of your learner's views and responses and be open to possibilities
- See difference as a creative space for enquiry and see where it takes you

---

Strength versus deficit

The project actively located itself within an anti-ableist paradigm, naming it structurally and acknowledging that this was the approach:

Over the last few years there has been increasing recognition for the concept of Neurodiversity, or variety in the ways in which our brains and neurology are different. This is leading to wider acceptance that people with recognised and diagnosed conditions such as autism and learning 'disabilities' have enormous learning potential that can be leveraged by considering them differently than those considered as 'neurotypical'. Another implication arising from embracing neurodiversity is increased validation for perceived learning and character strengths, as opposed to deficits. This confers many new opportunities for strength-based learning for Special Needs learners.

(Taken from the Open City evaluation)

Planning the project

Plan collectively and build flex and contingency

Planning is approached collectively and is based on prior knowledge of the learner; this informs how and in what way the project/curriculum could be accessed and guides how it can be facilitated in an appropriate and meaningful way. Planning offers a space to operate in and creates a context to support and further the learning for the student. It is important to view this as a creative space and one where you are answering questions, posing questions, and learning collectively. Planning is not something to be strictly adhered to – it is not punitive but instead supports teaching and learning.

Top tips

Co-production and understanding the spirit of inclusive anti-ableist pedagogy

1. Ensure that getting to know you is an objective and be curious about the learners and all those involved; acknowledge them; see them!
2. Ensure when you plan that it has flex and contingency and space to adapt to the learners' needs
3. Plan your first session based on the knowledge of the learners and the context of the project; how might they access it in a motivating and meaningful way?
4. Observe and look for opportunities to extend and form the learning around the student; be creative

★ If adopting an ipsative approach to assessment, this can be your baseline and inform your description of the learner.

Shaping an anti-ableist approach to pedagogy

The following diagram illustrates how this approach can be supported. It would be useful to share it with all involved so that there is a shared common understanding of it.

The diagram demonstrates how these three key components combine to support an inclusive and anti-ableist approach to pedagogy; the Venn diagram demonstrates how they are interlinked.

Knowledge of the learner and their active participation

The learner and the teacher have an equitable relationship that is reciprocal in nature. The teacher facilitates and presents the knowledge and skills and provides and plans the experiences, but both are protagonists and the teacher responds and extends the learning to mediate the entry points into the curriculum/project/body of knowledge. This reciprocity also means the teacher learns as part of the dynamic.

Personalised entry point

Creative entry points are negotiated that support and extend learning.

The intervention

The direct teaching happens when you marry these points and form them around the learner and co-construct the learning as a response to student voice, which informs you of the most appropriate way the learner can meaningfully access and participate in the learning.

Anti-ableist pedagogy is when these areas are facilitated.

Creativity and anti-ableist pedagogy

The spaces described and illustrated in the diagram are creative spaces. It is a useful exercise to anchor the phrase creativity within a definition that can give a shared common understanding. The following definition is taken from the All Our Futures report that was written by the late Sir Ken Robinson and seeks to describe some of the characteristics of creativity.

> Creativity is itself a mode of learning. It is distinctive in the combination of three features: a. It involves a thoughtful playfulness – learning through experimental 'play'. It is serious play conjuring up, exploring and developing possibilities and then critically evaluating and testing them. b. It involves a special flexibility in which there may be a conscious attempt to challenge the assumptions and preconceptions of the self – an unusual activity in which there is an active effort to unlearn in order to learn afresh. c. This process is driven by the need to find, introduce, construct or reconstruct something new. It seeks actively to expand the possibilities of any situation. In this sense the learning of creative thought is not neutral; it has a bias towards the innovative.
>
> (Taken from All Our Futures: Creativity, Culture and Education,
> Report to the Secretary of State for Education and Employment
> the Secretary of State for Culture, Media and Sport, May 1999:172)

The creative 'space' gives opportunity for learners and teachers to play, explore, and experiment. It allows for the pursuit of seeing different, of viewing the world through a different lens.

A creative, divergent space

This definition and the idea of difference, difference of experience and difference of viewpoint, of seeing and to 'learn afresh' chimes with those whose bodies and minds do not conform to notions of normalcy. Here creativity is located within a divergent and inclusive space.

It is also important that when referring to definitions or descriptors that they are used to support your understanding so that you articulate the learning in the spirit of these descriptors. They are to be interpreted and made real and given specificity; they are tools to support you and your articulation of creativity and are not to be used literally. It is the narration and the description of how and in what way the learning was creative that gives it meaning.

Developing an inclusive evaluative framework

This information informed a series of small activities that were designed to allow the artist, the musician, the class team, and the facilitator to get to know each of the learners and to then use this information to inform how the project would develop. This approach can also be seen as 'baselining' the students. This then gave a marker from which the learning developed; this type of assessment is ipsative and based on personal performance.

The information garnered at the beginning of the project was key in developing an evaluation framework. This inclusive framework located the student and student voice firmly at the centre of the planning and the assessment process to ensure that learning was meaningful and appropriate and would maximise the impact of the student's experience. This also helped to capture the learning journey and guided the project's development. Multiple entry points into the built environment were identified, and these approaches were being determined by the learners' responses and interests. The responses informed how the project unfolded, and this became a creative space.

Top tips

- Use highly motivating activities and look for entry points
- Get curious, observe, respond, and extend the learning

The objective of the first day

Getting to know you was an overt objective, and the day was framed as a day to understand how each student could initially access the project as described earlier. Questions were posed to determine what prior learning students had. This observational day led to a series of discussions that pulled on the teacher's knowledge, the way in which the students engaged with activities, and conversations with the class team and the artist facilitators. Here, innovation and creativity were used to high impact!

The facilitators had previous experience of working with each other and worked in a way that could be described as performance, process, and improvisations (see chapter 9 on contemporary art practice to see how these principles can support inclusion). Learning was anticipated but not static, and a creative conversation was being mediated in the project. The way they used their specific approach is explored later.

Material curiosity

The approach of celebrating the uniqueness of each response and supplying a range of materials to engage with allowed the participants benefit of starting their learning form their individual interest and cognitive need.

(Taken from the Open City evaluation)

New and interesting materials were introduced to the students. These materials were identified by the artists and then carefully presented; the artist would model their use and encourage the students to become 'curious' about their qualities and their potential for exploration. This allowed for a diversity of explorations and interpretations, and this gave space and allowed the students the time to become confident and use the materials within their artistic enquiry. Material entry points, the symbolic use of materials, and what they referred to was acknowledged and built upon – students' visual language was 'seen' and built upon with a diversity of outcomes as illustrated later.

Phenomenology

Phenomenology is the study of individuals' lived experience of the world, their subjective experience. By being **curious** about this and how experiences are subjectively lived, it can help to inform us, or reorient how we view or understand that experience. Presenting materials and the student's experience and response to these, of touching, manipulating, and feeling a material, the student's connection to it and how it made them feel were also honoured. The student's subjective reading allowed for this diversity of thinking that placed it firmly within a creative paradigm, allowing them to explore and experience and respond at their own pace.

Top tips

- Get curious (again!)
- Keep a constant dialogue, what's happening, what is that telling you?
- Introduce new ways of working and new materials – present them and give time and space for enquiry

---

A space to be, a space to learn . . .

Creating a space for change; learning as transformational

> Workshops were designed and facilitated with curiosity about each learner and the different ways in which they approach the discovery and experience of architecture.
>
> (Taken from the Open City evaluation)

One aspect was also creating a space for learning to happen; this could be described as the classroom climate. The learning space was less classroom with its association of hierarchy and didacticism and more collective enquiry and what could be described as studio practice, with the child as artist. Here the students were engaging in creative exploration.

Top tips

- Consider music as an accompaniment/cross art, how music can affect mood and facilitate learning
- Consider spaces and places in the room where students can direct their own learning, such as paper on the wall and they choose the tools that they would like to explore and work with

Cross arts

It is important to point out that the approach here was cross arts. The workshop was designed so that both art and music were happening within the same space; this chimed with a contemporary approach to art practice. The practitioners offered an alternative way of making art as they hadn't experienced the orthodoxy of teaching and were more attuned to their own practice. The approach was collaborative between the artist and the musician where music was used in a quiet and unobtrusive way to welcome and create sounds and spaces around activities. This responding to and building a climate of creativity and of acknowledging the student led to the formation of an environment where not only was creative enquiry taking place, but also a creative conversation around the students that was different to their usual experience. This approach was like that of studio practice and performance art. Learning and creativity flowing seamlessly.

What it is

> My workshop leading along with bassoon, electronics, voice, and body are being used to respond to the children and create held spaces where the children can: arrive, settle, relax, experience, explore, create, interact, play, be supported, work individually, come together as a group, extend ideas, celebrate, transition and play with ideas and materials relating to architecture and the built environment.
>
> (Luke Crookes, musician's evaluation report)

Student as artist

Impromptu display/celebration were site specific and improvised to draw out and pay attention to what was happening to reflect, share, and celebrate. Learning was made overt, and the creativity was noted and built upon to great effect.

Co-constructed learning

Learning was drawn out and sequenced and extended alongside the student. This chimes with the Vygotskian notion of the more experienced other, or scaffolding, and that knowledge is culturally generated.

Implications

The implications of this approach to pedagogy are significant for all those involved. There was an increased engagement from all protagonists involved within the project. Increased engagement from the students, with them actively requesting to have more 'art', and positive affectations were observed. This was also noted amongst the class team, and the implications were wider. The artists reported that the project with its creative and improvised approach also made them consider their own practice, helped them develop confidence in their approach to pedagogy, and gave them contingency in their practice.

The following images are from the project and illustrate the breadth and range of artistic enquiry.

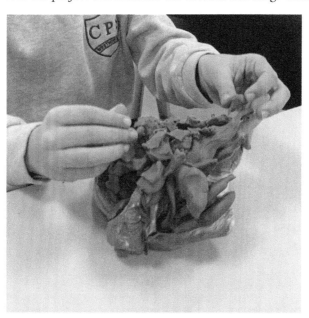

Image 8.1 Student hands and plasticine

Image 8.2 Student hands and plasticine

Exploring and experiencing materials such as plasticine. With the subjective experience of being present and responding to these materials, the phenomenological experience was acknowledged and was part of the learning and informed how the project could develop for the students.

The following images illustrate a creative enquiry that moves across a range of media and demonstrate how the outcomes of this enquiry are wide ranging. This diversity demonstrates how the project facilitated each individual student, engaging them at their point of entry into the project and how their creative enquiry evolved. The images demonstrate an articulation within their enquiry that was sensitively facilitated and championed by the artists and the musician and the project's structure.

Image 8.3 Clay tile form with holes in it

Image 8.4 Painted clay tile form with holes in it

Image 8.5 Painted clay form

Image 8.6 Painting of a helicopter

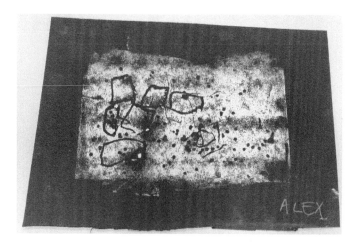

Image 8.7 Black-and-white print

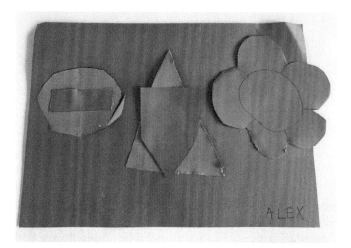

Image 8.8 Blue and orange paper collage

Image 8.9 Clay sculpture with wooden sticks

Image 8.10 Clay and polystyrene sculpture of a bus

These two diverse outcomes again demonstrate an anti-ableist approach. The 3D investigations that the students made show a playfulness. Image 8.10 is a representation of a bus and within its construction is the implicit and discreet mathematical skills of ratio and spatial relationship. Image 8.9 involves spatial relationship and an emerging sense of 3D composition with elements referring to each other to make a 3D sculptural piece.

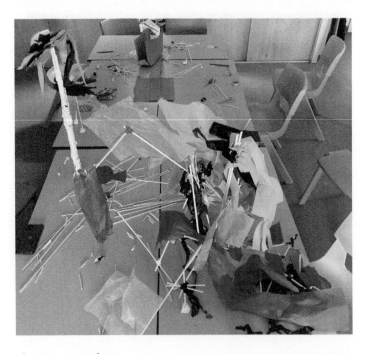

Image 8.11 Tissue paper and paper straw sculpture

Image 8.12 Tissue paper sculpture

Image 8.13 Tissue paper and wire sculpture

Concluding notes

This chapter has explored some of the principles of anti-ableist pedagogy in a case study. It examined how this approach was developed through the professional dialogue that accompanied this approach. It shows how the dynamics of the student and teacher's relationship developed over time to be collaborative, leading to co-constructed learning where the young person was fully included. It was conducted within a school setting but alongside cultural partners. It highlights the importance of co-production and how this led to increased engagement and increased impact. This is a theme that is explored again in chapter 11 and mentioned in chapter 10 and demonstrates its importance within inclusion and inclusive practices.

Impromptu installations and celebrations of the student's collective enquiry supported the studio-based approach and their active involvement in the learning. This collective installation approach and its immediacy also supported the idea of a creative community of learners.

Characteristics of anti-ableist pedagogy

- There is a broad and inclusive range of cultural references that are being promoted and used to contextualise learning; drawing on artists who are also D/deaf, disabled, and neurodivergent and from different ethnic and socioeconomic backgrounds
- Planning supports learning and anticipates need, but creates a framework to teach within that has flexibility
- Process is valued and the journey of learning given status
- The student is located centrally within the teaching
- Differences in being, seeing, and experiencing are seen as assets and offer creative opportunities for enquiry
- There are multiple entry points into the curriculum/project, and these are informed by the students
- Learning is co-constructed, and the student is fully acknowledged and is central within this process
- Assessment is qualitative in approach and tells the story of the students learning using both ipsative and narrative assessment
- Diversity of outcomes illustrate a structurally inclusive and anti-ableist approach to pedagogy
- Introduce everyone and be clear about their roles
- Understand what co-production is, describe it and how you have structurally embedded it within the project/pedagogy, and give its status
- Ensure shared common language and understanding of the objectives
- Use an ipsative assessment model, pertinent and descriptive of the student's entry points to their learning
- Make time for and give value to evaluations; these can be informal conversations
- Name the way you have chosen to work – co-produced learning – and give it status
- Inclusive person-centric approaches are also anti-ableist
- Be curious of your learner's views and responses and be open to possibilities
- See difference as a creative space for enquiry and see where it takes you
- Ensure that getting to know you is an objective and be curious about the learners and all those involved; acknowledge them; see them!
- Ensure when you plan that it has flex and contingency and space to adapt to the learners' needs
- Plan your first session based on the knowledge of the learner and the context of the project; how might they access it in a motivating and meaningful way?
- Observe and looks for opportunities to extend and form the learning around the student; be creative
- Use highly motivating activities and look for entry points
- Get curious, observe, respond, and extend the learning
- Keep a constant dialogue, what's happening, what is that telling you?
- Introduce new ways of working and new materials – present them and give time and space for enquiry
- Consider music as an accompaniment/cross art, how music can affect mood and facilitate learning
- Consider spaces and places in the room where students can direct their own learning, such as paper on the wall and they choose the tools that they would like to explore and work with

---

References

All Our Futures: Creativity, Culture and Education, Report to the Secretary of State for Education and Employment the Secretary of State for Culture, Media and Sport, May 1999.
All images in this chapter courtesy of Open City

Useful information

National Society for Education in Art and Design (NSEAD)

www.nsead.org

Critical pedagogy

bell hooks

bell hooks has written a number of books on education, but I would heartily recommend *Teaching Community* and *Teaching to Transgress*.

Paulo Freire

A leading advocate of the critical pedagogy theory and author of the influential *Pedagogy of the Oppressed*.

9 Contemporary art practice and inclusive art practice

In this chapter we explore the commonalities between inclusive practice and contemporary art practice as a means of describing an inclusive approach to pedagogy.

Some of the characteristics of contemporary art practice align with inclusive arts education and offer an alternative way to access, make, and experience art. This approach creates and moves away from the orthodoxy of typical art production in schools that sometimes has been described as 'school art'. Contemporary art practice offers new and legitimate entry points and approaches to making art. This chapter also considers inclusive assessment and how it can be used to support inclusive teaching and learning.

How to use this chapter

This chapter will briefly explore some of the cultural shifts that supported the development of contemporary art practice, articulating their commonalities with inclusive pedagogy. It considers the notion of child as artist, uses examples of student artwork as exemplars of these commonalities, and examines the work of two artists and describes a range of entry points to their work.

Contemporary art practice offers a different approach to pedagogy where we can explore the notion of multiple entry points to art practice, all of which are legitimate and non-hierarchical. Within this new subjective and legitimising pedagogy all students can engage in, experience, respond to, and make art that can be described as meaningful, appropriate, and contemporary.

Using contemporary artists to inform teaching and learning

In this chapter we will be looking at three contemporary artists: Yinka Shonibare, Linda Bell, and Nnena Kalu. I have intentionally chosen these artists because they identify firstly as artists, but they also have a disability, all are currently practising artists. The intention of this was to support the concept of the inclusive canon as mentioned in chapter 6 on disability-led and disability-focused organisations and to increase the visibility of artists that also identify as having a disability and to be reflective of the young disabled people that we teach.

Directory of artists

A directory of D/deaf, disabled, and neurodivergent artists appears at the end of the chapter to use as examples or for further enquiry.

Entry points identified

The artist's work is examined, their characteristics identified, and concepts explored within their practice. Multiple entry points to their work are articulated through a mapping activity that would meet the needs of a range of learners accessing various curriculum pathways. These entry points offer a starting point and points of departure for both lateral exploration and linear exploration.

To understand this exploration, it is helpful to look at the idea of learning and how that relates to notions of progression and how it also corresponds to skills, knowledge, and the curriculum.

Concept of learning: how it works

Skills

Skills are the acquisition of abilities through practice and rehearsal. They are developed in specific situations through a combination of sensory input and output. They are developed over time and are practically based and refined through trial and error.

DOI: 10.4324/9781003122258-9

Knowledge

Knowledge is the information that is acquired through sensory input such as watching, touching, listening, and reading. Knowledge refers to the information and the theoretical concepts that are acquired through these activities. Knowledge can be acquired through direct teaching, the knowledge transmitted from one person to another and that chimes with the Vygotskian concept of the more experienced other and scaffolding. Knowledge can also be self-acquired through reading and observation.

The distinction between knowledge and skills is that knowledge is theoretical and skills are practical.

Curriculum

This refers to the subjects and the context in which the knowledge and skills are located, the subjects and the course of study.

Learning and progression; cognition and cognitive generalisation

Cognition is the mental function of acquiring knowledge. It describes a process where this knowledge is generated through thought, experiences, and senses. Memory formation is a key factor within this construct and is something that we will explore briefly in the chapter. Cognitive generalisation is the ability to apply this knowledge across a number of different contexts and progression is described through engagement. This is explored later in the chapter.

Lateral exploration and progression

Lateral exploration takes place when a student explores a concept over time through repetition and rehearsal. The student explores this concept within different settings to support their cognition. Here the progression is lateral as the learning is generalising the one concept across a number of different situations.

Linear exploration and progression

Linear progression describes the acquisition of skills and knowledge that is built upon and further developed in a linear and upward trajectory of development. The rate of progress is faster, and the concepts learnt become more sophisticated as the acquired knowledge is further added to and the skills increase over time.

Curriculum pathways

Next, I briefly describe the various curriculum pathways that you would find in both special schools and mainstream settings and the characteristics of learning that take place in these pathways. The descriptions are for signposting purposes only; these curriculum pathways are not fixed, as movement between the different pathways does take place.

Pre-formal curriculum

This is the pathway for learners who have profound and multiple learning difficulties (PMLD). Students are mostly wheelchair users, have physical disabilities and complex medical needs, and have profound developmental delay. The learners here make profoundly slow progress, and the learning is often through sensory and/or experiential activities. Learning here is often improvised and is based on the students' affectations and responses to stimuli and historical knowledge of these (pupil centred). All communication is nonverbal, and knowledge of the learner is essential for meaningful activities to be offered. Progress may be lateral and static in nature with a focus on quality of experience.

Informal curriculum

The informal curriculum is focused on active exploration and works within a play-based paradigm where students are 'learning to be, rather than learning to do'. The curriculum will have lots of sensory activities that facilitate active engagement and communication, expressing needs and wants, and may have learners that are both verbal with limited language and nonverbal. The curriculum, like that of the pre-formal, is tailored to the needs of the learner (pupil centred); progression will often be lateral in nature and the focus will be on generalising learning through rehearsal and repetition. Students will require visual supports and communication aides.

Semi-formal curriculum

The semi-formal has aspects of the informal such as sensory and exploratory, but learners will make linear progress, although the rate of progression will be slow. The generalisation will be supported through rehearsal and repetition. There might be more progress in the acquisition of skills than knowledge. Again, students will require visual supports and communication aides.

Formal

Learning over time is subject specific and the progress is linear in nature and faster. Students may require visual supports and communication aides.

Memory formation and learning

A key consideration when teaching students who are working within the pre-formal and informal curriculum pathways is the ability to form memory. The formation of memory will aid them in their ability to recall and learn. Multisensory teaching supports memory formation by using the sensory pathways to increase the chances of a memory being formed. There are different types of memory; two of these are episodic and procedural.

Episodic memory

Sensory experiences trigger episodic memories which are subjective.

These memories are experiential; they are attached to an experience and an individual and can also be described as emotive. They chime with the notion of person centred and are person specific.

Procedural memory

This memory is an automatic memory and is based on skill, like tying your shoelaces or knowing how to ride a bike. It is described as an unconscious and long-term memory that supports particular tasks.

Multisensory teaching

This form of teaching uses the various sensory pathways to engage and stimulate neurons and strengthen neural pathways. Neurons are the nerve cells that receive sensory input from the external world. They are used to send motor commands to our muscles and for transforming and relaying the electrical signals at every stage between. Sensory integration is how we use this information to form perceptions of the world around us and what is happening. This perception then informs the memories that we make.

The following diagram shows how both long-term memory and working/sensory memory can be supported.

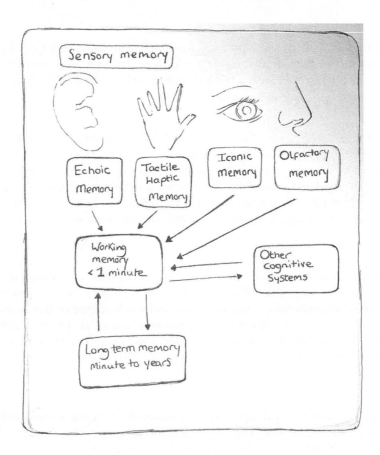

Image 9.1 Diagram showing different memory formations

Source: Based on a diagram found in Chatterjee, H (2008) *Touch in Museums*, page 167.

Working memory

Working memory is the part of short-term memory which is concerned with immediate conscious perceptual and linguistic processing.

Long-term memory

This term describes the type of memory responsible for the storage of information for an extended period of time. The development of this type of memory can support the generalisation of concepts.

Inclusive pedagogy and contemporary art practice

Inclusive pedagogy in the space of arts and culture has similar characteristics to those found in contemporary art practice. The following diagram explores some of these characteristics. These can also be located within classroom practice and offer a framework for this enquiry. Thediagram below describes some of the characteristics of contemporary art practice

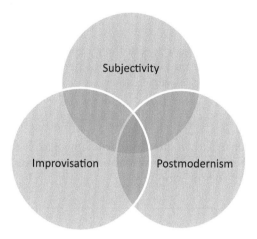

Subjectivity

Within education, practitioners and students bring their own experience, perceptions, and specificity into the classroom. This subjectivity can make learning potent; this is often described in two ways as student voice and person centred/person centric. Student voice refers to the acknowledgement of the learner's voice, where it is heard. It directly informs and impacts on their learning so that they are active participants and help to co-construct their learning. Within special needs teaching the notion of subjectivity can relate directly to the idea of person-centred learning. This is where the learning is formed around the learner in direct relation to both their specific needs and what they engage with and find motivating. Engagement is a central tenet of inclusion and inclusive practice and refers to the context of the learning; engagement can be used as an entry point into a wider curriculum area.

Within contemporary art practice subjectivity and the human condition are areas that are readily explored. This chimes with the postmodern notion of many narratives, multiple readings, and multiple entry points. This can be seen within many different strands of contemporary art that explore issues and personal narratives and invite the viewer to actively participate and co-construct meaning.

Improvisation

Some contemporary art practices have elements of improvisation, performance, and participation. They can be seen particularly within the field of *performance art* and the fleeting nature of 'in the moment' actions and the relationship that is developed between the performer and the viewer. Immersive art experiences are also found within installation art. Responses can be constructed and generated by both the artist through their interpretation of spaces and the viewer through this interpretation and response to these actions and spaces. Within education, and more specifically assessment for learning (AfL), can be found an approach where improvised teaching occurs and where learning is formed around the learner based on the feedback on where they are within their learning. It also aligns with the Vygotskian social constructivist notion of the more experienced other and the concept of scaffolding.

Postmodern, modernism, and the parallels of integration and inclusion

Postmodernism within art practice acknowledges that there are many narratives and multiple entry points to making, viewing, and experiencing art. It challenges the notion that there is a right way to view, make, and experience art.

Postmodernism can be seen in opposition to modernism. Modernism was essentially a post-war vision of progress and science that permeated all of society. There were issues with its all-encompassing approach, a philosophy that was developed after the Second World War and constructed through a patriarchal, white Eurocentric lens. This led to a very specific notion and uniformity around principles of art and cultural production. After the war, society was rebuilding and reconceptualising itself after the horrors experienced, and progress and notions of a futuristic society driven by science became prominent in society. Here is where tensions exist. By placing a singular model, a metanarrative of conformity, on society where a corresponding value judgement was attached, a preferred culture and cultural production became dominant. Earlier in the book I described the concept of normalcy and the idea that society has been constructed with a specific vision of what constitutes normal. Here modernism supported a uniform idea, and any deviation from this could be viewed as a deficit. This can be seen to support the notion of integration, integration to a perceived notion of normality. This chimes with the medical model of disability, to be 'fixed' and then integrated into society.

I would suggest that this firmly locates integration within the wider paradigm of modernism. Postmodern theory aligns itself much more with those non-hierarchical and democratic characteristics of inclusion and inclusive practice and the many non-conforming bodies and minds that exist within society.

Using contemporary artists; mapping entry points

Next, we have located these ideas within the practices of three contemporary artists to use them as the basis for a scheme of work and artistic enquiry. For the purposes of this mapping exercise, we will highlight entry points in reference to the four curriculum pathways as described earlier.

The national curriculum

The overarching aims of the national curriculum shown in the following table state quite clearly that students should **produce creative work** and that they should also **learn about great artists**. These artists create a useful context from which to do this in a meaningful and inclusive way.

Aims

The national curriculum for art and design aims to ensure that all pupils:

- Produce creative work, exploring their ideas and recording their experiences
- Become proficient in drawing, painting, sculpture, and other art, craft, and design techniques
- Evaluate and analyse creative works using the language of art, craft, and design
- Know about great artists, craft makers, and designers and understand the historical and cultural development of their art forms (National Curriculum in England, 2014:225)

The child as artist: free drawing or painting and the promotion of creativity

In the majority of my lessons that have structured activities, I always allow time for students to make their own art. I describe this as 'free drawing or painting', and it usually happens at the end of the session. This allows the students to make creative choices and to be empowered through them. It also gives students autonomy and agency in the art room and helps to promote a sense of self. These self-directed activities give students the opportunity to fully realise and communicate their creative voice and to explore issues that are pertinent to themselves. These outcomes have as much value as the structured activity and give voice to the child as an artist, and they should be celebrated as such.

Mapping points of entry to contemporary artists

In the following tables, I have looked at three contemporary artists and their practice and mapped ways in which they can be used to inform curriculum.

How to use the tables

In the tables, I have mapped entry points to the artwork of Nnena Kalu, Yinka Shonibare, and Linda Bell. These are organised in reference to the various curriculum pathways and correspond to them. However, these are only suggestions and the activities in the different curriculum pathways could be similar, just accessed differently. I have added a rationale and also possible learning objectives. As there is a lot of crossover, I have elaborated more in some curriculum pathways and then referenced them in others so as not to replicate information. The learning objectives outlined are specific to the activities, but these activities may also support the students in working towards the outcomes outlined in their EHC plans.

Nnena Kalu

Image 9.2 Nnena Kalu

Source: Image courtesy of ActionSpace

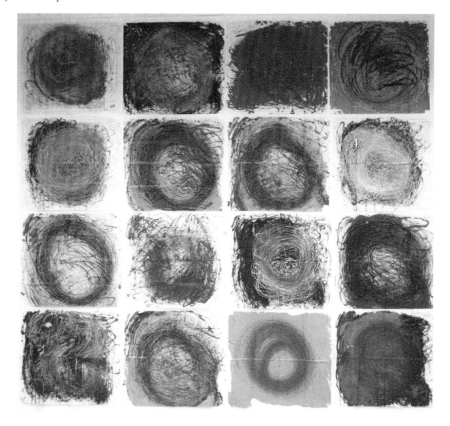

Image 9.3 Photograph of a large sculpture by Nnena Kalu

Source: Image courtesy of ActionSpace

Image 9.2 is from Nnena's first major London-based solo commission for 'elsewhere', Studio Voltaire's offsite programme in 2020, and the image to the below is from the maps series of works. All images are courtesy of ActionSpace.

Curriculum pathways	Entry points to Nnena Kalu	Notes on process/ product/vocabulary and assessment	Vocabulary	Value added
Pre-formal learning objectives: To access sensory and experiential activities that are person centred and where the entry point is based on prior knowledge of the learner	**Making spaces** **Rationale:** Making an installation over time that directly references the work of the artist Nnena Kalu. Building the installation through a process of exploration that is both sensory and experiential. Making the installation through processes by adding and layering them into the installation over time. This also supports the notion of art as social practice, building the installation as a shared activity and experience. Attaching the materials as they are explored and then collectively exploring the installation as a sense of place and as a record of these activities. **Touch/haptic exploration:** Wrapping and co-building structures that affix to the ceiling or a pre-built structure or a hula hoop. Building, touching, and exploring different textures and different weights of materials. Sheer, see-through and heavy fabrics and fabrics of different colours: bright, metallic, fluorescent, and so on. Using coloured sticky tape to bind these so that they are secure. Hanging ribbons from above, these could be blown and operated by a switch, or a leaf blower or fan, and students could track and anticipate the movement, or use switches to turn fans on, supporting their understanding of cause and effect. Encasing objects by wrapping them in ribbons and hanging them. Making containers or using plastic bottles to hang and adding smells and materials that will make sounds such as rice and lentils. Exploring these in trays, their textures the sounds they make and through this exploration adding them to the containers and shaking them. Making them through a process of exploration and then attaching them to the sculpture, then exploring the 'space' that the sculpture then describes through these sounds, smells, and textures. This installation could then remain and become part of the sensory landscape of the classroom. **Modroc or papier-mâché a balloon and add a smell:** Touching and feeling inflated balloons, watching them being blown up and feeling the air move as they deflate. Tracking movement as they fly around the room and hear the sound that they make. Adding lentils or rice to the balloons so that they make sounds as they are touched and move. Adding more balloons and making a collection of these as part of the installation.	**Process:** Case studies that could be a series of images and notes describing the engagement over time; narrative assessment of how and in which way the student engaged. **Product:** The sculpture itself as a 'product'.	n/a	Links to SMSC

Curriculum pathways	Entry points to Nnena Kalu	Notes on process/product/vocabulary and assessment	Vocabulary	Value added
	Using Modroc or papier-mâché, exploring it dry and as it changes when water is applied, smoothing the Modroc together, hand over hand together over the balloon. Building and layering this over a series of weeks, adding textures and smells such as cloves and dried herbs and encasing these. Remember to add in string or ribbons when you are adding the Modroc to help you to attach the balloon to the sculpture. Once these are completed, paint could be added again as a shared activity, promoting choice making through gestures and eye gaze. Paint could be added from above and tracked and sponges could be used to support physically painting the balloons. **Ribbons and herbs:** As you wrap, explore smells, and add these to the installation as you progress, wrap sprigs of rosemary and lavender, smell these and tie them with ribbons, touch the ribbons, exploring the texture, and wave the ribbon from above, track the movements. Once you have wrapped your herbs add them to the installation. **Fluorescent paint:** Fabrics and ribbons could also transform the sculpture by using UV lights and could again extend the students' experience of the space.			
Informal learning objectives: • To actively explore materials • To make choices and request materials • To work in 2D • To work in 3D	**Rationale:** Making an installation over time that directly references the work of Nnena Kalu. Building the installation through the process of active exploration. Making an installation of these processes by adding and layering them into an installation over time. Building an installation through collective social practice art practice, attaching the materials as they are explored and collectively exploring the installation as a sense of place. To also make 2D art as response to Nnena Kalu's map series. ★ Elements of the pre-formal entry points will also be relevant and could be used to support learning. **Painting and making marks on materials to be used as wrapping:** Painting on plastic, like clear shower curtains or plastic sheets from builders' yards. Recycling materials; environmentalism – recycling and reusing and the democratic use of materials, i.e., easily accessible. Using a range of sized brushes, sponges, and rollers to offer choice, adding and mixing colours, choosing colours by requesting and gesturing, and adding other materials to extend interest such as glitter and glue. **Physically exploring textures and materials and tape through active exploration and making an object:** By growing, building, connecting by taping, scrunching materials, ripping, and physically engaging in material exploration. Using coloured tape to bind these materials together.	**Process:** Case studies that could be a series of images and notes describing the engagement over time; narrative assessment of how and in which way the student engaged. **Product:** The sculpture itself as a 'product'.		Links to SMSC

Curriculum pathways	Entry points to Nnena Kalu	Notes on process/ product/vocabulary and assessment	Vocabulary	Value added
	Exploring and making containers to hang: Exploring materials that could be placed in containers that could make sounds, for example exploring different coloured rice and pasta in a tray. Pouring and adding to containers by using a funnel, using different sized containers, shaking them and hanging them, then swinging them to make sounds. **Mark making on found objects; relating to Nnena Kalu's map series:** Mark making on found objects like maps. Movement and drawing as a response to music using a range of media, pens, pencils, pastels, various sizes to support various dexterities. ★ Wheelchairs making marks with movements and making drawing devices links to Rebecca Horn's drawing machines. **Exploring ribbons:** Exploring their movement aspects of performance, moving, swaying, binding, wrapping objects. Favourite objects like Lego or toys that could be used within the installation.			
Semi-formal learning objectives: • To respond to the work of an artist • To actively explore materials • To use tools appropriately and with intention, i.e., pencil and paintbrushes • To make art/ mark making as a response to music • To work in 2D • To work in 3D	**Rationale:** Making an installation over time that directly references the work of Nnena Kalu. Building the installation through the process of active exploration and developing skills in relation to sculpture and actively making decisions. Being introduced to the concept of the artists and giving basic biographical information such as their name. To develop 2D work as a response to Nnena's maps series of work and mark making onto found imagery. **Mark making onto found imagery:** This could take the form of mark making and adding to the student's favourite cartoon characters, appropriating this imagery into their own work. This can also be hugely motivating. The mark making could also be on top of the work of Nnena Kalu's work and the students could be appropriating her work into their own. Offering a range of media to promote choice and independence. **Mark making to music:** Listening to different types of music and seeing how it makes the students feel, how does it affect the way in which they make marks, considering fast, slow, soft, and hard and again using a range of media. **Balloon sculptures:** As previously mentioned, they could be covered either in Modroc or papier-mâché and painted and could be added, bound together using tape, and suspended from the ceiling. **Binding sculptures:** Using ribbons as previously mentioned to explore and bind and gather objects together. This could also link to the artist Judith Scott, see table at the end of the chapter.	**Process:** Case studies that could be a series of images and notes describing the engagement over time; narrative assessment of how and in which way the student engaged and the development of skills and understanding of art practice. **Product:** The sculpture itself as a 'product'.	**Communication via communication aids for requesting and choice making** 2D 3D Appropriate Art Artist Balloon Colours Colouring Drawing Fabric Found imagery Gluing Mixed media Painting Ribbon Sculpture	Links to SMSC

Curriculum pathways	Entry points to Nnena Kalu	Notes on process/product/vocabulary and assessment	Vocabulary	Value added
Formal learning objectives: • To make work as a response to an artist • To have some biographical understanding of the artist and their work • To work in 2D • To work in 3D • To produce work following a process • To produce work that is immediate • To use art-specific terminology	**Rationale:** Making an installation over time that directly references the work of Nnena Kalu. Building the installation through the process of active exploration. Making an installation of these processes by adding and layering them into an installation over time. Building an installation through collective social art practice, attaching the materials as they are explored and collectively exploring the installation as a sense of place. To develop an understanding of an artists practice, to gain familiarity with their work and be able to name the artist and describe some of the characteristics of their work and start developing an understanding of their practice as a response to the artists' work. To develop a sculpture over time following a sequence of activities and processes to realise a piece: the sculpture. To produce work that is immediate and to also use art specific vocabulary appropriately. **Mark making onto found imagery:** As outlined previously. Encourage the use of art-specific language such as found object and appropriation. **Balloon sculptures:** As previously mentioned, they could be covered in either Modroc or papier-mâché and painted and could be added, bound together using tape, and suspended from the ceiling. **Binding sculptures:** Using ribbons as previously mentioned to explore and bind and gather objects together. This could also link to the artist Judith Scott; see table at the end of the chapter.	**Process:** Case studies that could be a series of images and notes describing the engagement over time; narrative assessment of how and in which way the student engaged and the development of skills and understanding of art practice. **Product:** The sculpture itself as a 'product'.	**Communication via communication aids for requesting and choice making** 2D 3D Appropriate Art Artist Balloon Colours Colouring Drawing Fabric Found imagery Gluing Mixed media Painting Ribbon Sculpture	Links to SMSC

Yinka Shonibare

Image 9.4 Image of Yinka Shonibare's *Nelson's Boat in a Bottle* artwork.

Source: Image courtesy of Shonibare Studio

Curriculum pathways	Entry points to Yinka Shonibare; with specific links to Nelson's ship in a bottle	Notes on process/ product/vocabulary and assessment	Vocabulary	Value added
Pre-formal learning objectives: To access sensory and experiential activities that are person centred and where the entry point is based on prior knowledge of the learner	**Making spaces** **Rationale:** To use Yinka Shonibare's artwork as a context to support creative exploration. To use the subject and material qualities of his artwork as an impetus for further enquiry. To use his work to promote both sensory and experiential activities and explore the idea of different places in relation to identity. **Boats, travelling between Africa and Europe stations, sensory stations:** Exploring the idea of travelling and movement, using wheelchairs to travel between two places. One station would represent Africa and the other Europe. Each station could have a different smell. The African station could have herbs such as cloves and cinnamon sticks and the European station herbs such as rosemary and thyme. **Travelling between the stations:** Using iridescent blue and white fabrics to simulate a journey taken by sea. The iridescent fabrics could be pulled over the wheelchairs to immerse the student or held above in a similar fashion to the parachute game. Water sprays that have a small amount of salt could be sprayed in the air to simulate sea spray. Boats could be used to accompany the chairs between the two stations, or chairs could have sails added to them to make them boat-like using batik fabric. The batik fabric could also be cut into large triangles that look like the sails of a ship; these could also be loose and hung from the ceiling if possible. The sound of sea gulls could accompany the journey and rain sticks could be used as a means of simulating a storm at sea. Heavy ropes could be used like rigging and laid over the students, allowing them to experience the ropes' weight. **Water and water play:** Water play using bubble bath and sensory sponges could be used at the end of activities as a means of cleaning up as well as a sensory activity. **Making boat sails; painting with feet onto canvas/fabric:** This could be a great activity for those students who spend a lot of time in wheelchairs as it allows them to haptically explore and experience an activity using a part of their body that isn't often exposed to many sensory experiences. Firstly, it's a good idea to warm the feet up with a massage with a fragrant cream so that they are receptive to the activity. Students who are following the pre-formal curriculum route will have profound delay, and this will inhibit their sensory processing, so this introductory activity should help to stimulate the nerve endings. The massage will support	**Process:** Case studies that could be a series of images and notes describing the engagement over time; narrative assessment of how and in which way the student engaged.	n/a	Links to SMSC

Curriculum pathways	Entry points to Yinka Shonibare; with specific links to Nelson's ship in a bottle	Notes on process / product / vocabulary and assessment	Vocabulary	Value added
	the student in being ready for the following painting activity. Before applying the paint, you could introduce the learner to the texture of the brush that you intend to use – large soft brushes are the most useful – and brush the feet for at least five minutes. You could then add the paint; you could offer two colours, holding them apart to see which the young person looks at and use this colour. You could add the paint to both the feet and to the canvas, and this could easily be manipulated around the students' feet. After you have competed the activity, a warm sensory foot wash using bubble bath followed by a foot massage could signify that the activity has ended. **Hand massage or foot massage:** In my own practice I use these a lot as a sensory cue to both start an activity and to end an activity. The massage could be accompanied by music.			
Informal learning objectives: • To actively explore materials • To make choices and request materials • To work in 2D • To work in 3D	**Rationale:** To use Yinka Shonibare's artwork as a context to support creative exploration. To use the qualities of his artwork as an impetus for further enquiry. To use his work to promote both sensory and experiential activities. To explore the narrative aspects of Yinka Shonibare's boat and the idea of multiculturalism and different identities. To use batik fabric, exploring its qualities and patterns; to physically explore the fabric in a playful manner on tables as students add paint. **Activities:** The activities here can be very similar to those identified for the pre-formal learners, however with the sail painting activity students could actively engage in the mark making and painting activities. Offer a range of mediums such as pencils or large chubby wax crayon. Students could also use a range of different sized brushes, sponges, and rollers to offer choice, adding and mixing colours. Students could choose colours by requesting and gesturing and adding other materials to extend interest such as glitter and glue.	**Process:** Case studies that could be a series of images and notes describing the engagement over time; narrative assessment of how and in which way the student engaged. **Product:** The painted fabric.		Links to SMSC
Semi-formal learning objectives: • To respond to the work of an artist • To introduce the concept of an artist • To actively explore materials • To identify basic shapes within a pattern • To name and request colours, materials, and tools • To use tools appropriately and with intention, i.e., pencil and paintbrushes	**Rationale:** To use Yinka Shonibare's artwork as a context to support creative exploration. To use the qualities of his artwork as an impetus for further enquiry. To use his work to promote both sensory and experiential activities. To explore the narrative aspects of Yinka Shonibare's boat and the idea of multiculturalism and different identities. To use batik fabric, exploring its qualities and patterns; to physically explore the fabric in a playful manner on tables as students add paint and appropriate and add to the batik to make their own ship sales. To introduce the students to an image of Yinka Shonibare and identify him as the artist.	**Process:** Case studies that could be a series of images and notes describing the engagement over time; narrative assessment of how and in which way the student engaged. **Product:** The sculpture itself as a 'product'.	**Communication via communication aids for requesting and choice making** Art Artist Balloon Colours Colouring Drawing Fabric Gluing Painting Ribbon	Links to SMSC

(Continued)

Curriculum pathways	Entry points to Yinka Shonibare; with specific links to Nelson's ship in a bottle	Notes on process/ product/vocabulary and assessment	Vocabulary	Value added
• To make art/ mark making as a response to music • To work in 2D • To work in 3D	**Activities:** The activities here can be very similar to those identified for the informal learners. With the focus on active engagement within the activities and the promotion of choice making, such as colours or selecting the tools the student would like to work with. **Patterns and shapes:** Oversized and simple patterns could be used in bold black lines and students encouraged to make marks on top of these. Shapes could also be taken from the batik fabric and cut out in card and the students could mark make and/or render on to these. These shapes could then be arranged by the teacher and reimagined into a batik pattern that could be displayed. Here there is the opportunity for the students to also name simple shapes within the fabric. **Making boats:** Using strong grey card cut two simple shapes that will resemble the hull of the boat. These could be painted using brown paint, or alternatively you could mix the three primary colours (red, yellow, and blue) to make brown as a cause-and-effect activity. Now using paper draw a sail-like shape – this is where the students could collage photocopied batik fabric to signify the sail. To construct the boat, you will need to glue a piece of balsa wood between the two pieces of card that resemble the hull and add a dowel or bamboo cane in between for the sail to be attached to.			
Formal learning objectives: • To make work as a response to an artist • To have some biographical understanding of the artist and their work • To work in 2D • To work in 3D • To produce work following a process • To produce work that is immediate • To use art-specific terminology	**Rationale:** To use Yinka Shonibare's artwork as a context to support creative exploration. To use the qualities of his artwork as an impetus for further enquiry. To use his work to promote both sensory and experiential activities. To explore the narrative aspects of Yinka Shonibare's boat and the idea of multiculturalism and different identities. To use batik fabric, exploring its qualities and patterns, to physically explore the fabric in a playful manner on tables as students add paint and appropriate the batik to make their own ship sails. To introduce the students to an image of Yinka Shonibare and identify him as the artist and to make connections between his work and theirs. This can also be used to support their understanding of diversity. **Activities:** The activities here can be very similar to those identified for the semi-formal learners, again with the focus on active engagement and choice making. There will be a focus on developing their work through a process and building on skills and knowledge and making links between their work and the work of Yinka Shonibare.	**Process:** Case studies that could be a series of images and notes describing the engagement over time; narrative assessment of how and in which way the student engaged. **Product:** The sculpture itself as a 'product'.	Art Artist Batik fabric Colours Collage Constructing Drawing Fabric Identity Painting Sculpture	Links to SMSC

Curriculum pathways	Entry points to Yinka Shonibare; with specific links to Nelson's ship in a bottle	Notes on process/ product/vocabulary and assessment	Vocabulary	Value added
	Patterns:			
	The patterns and the use of shapes can be explored as with the semi-formal entry point. The assemblage of the shapes into a pattern could be a group activity and could support choice making, turn taking, and negotiation in making a piece of collaborative art.			
	Boats:			
	The emphasis here could be on mixing a tertiary colour (brown) on to paper by mixing the three primary colours to represent wood. After these have dried, they could be collaged onto the shapes resembling the hull. The collaging of the sails could also mean a greater sense of control, and the students could also work with the teacher in using the glue gun in constructing the sculpture.			

Linda Bell

Image 9.5 Image of Linda Bell's sculpture

Source: Image courtesy of ActionSpace

Image 9.6 Photograph of Linda Bell's hanging sculpture

Source: Image courtesy of ActionSpace

Curriculum pathways	Entry points to Linda Bell's sculptural works	Notes on process/product/vocabulary and assessment	Vocabulary	Value added
Pre-formal learning objectives: To access sensory and experiential activities that are person centred and where the entry point is based on prior knowledge of the learner	**Sensory clouds and playful making Rationale:** To use Linda Bell's artwork as a context to support creative exploration. To use the material qualities of her artwork as an impetus for further enquiry. To use her work to promote both sensory and experiential activities and explore materials qualities and the idea of participatory arts and performance in making. **Playful making/participatory making:** Material curiosity, exploring a range of materials that are light in weight and have a tactile quality like netting, iridescent shredded paper and cotton wool, wool, ribbons, and feathers and organza fabric. Each of these could be touched, wrapped around the body, and explored before being used in the installations/assemblages outlined later. Improvised exploration dependent on how and in what way the student engages. The materials refashioned into hangings and groups. Using small sections of netting and metallic paper and ribbons that could be handled and explored in a number of ways such as visually from above and also for their tactile qualities. To extend the playful nature and the idea of participatory – mirrors could be used so that students can see themselves exploring the materials and materials could be wrapped around their hands etc. – the pressure giving them a whole-body experience. **Clouds/hangings installation:** Building sensory cloud sculptures using the approach mentioned earlier. These amorphous, moving clouds could be made from netting that could be purchased online or from haberdashers/textile shops. They could be hung from a washing line, or on a frame, inside or outside the classroom, or in the playground in the summer. Combining this with other sensory items such as wind chimes for sounds or pre-recorded sounds using sound buttons. Adding fairy lights inside the clouds so that there is a transformation – changing when the lights go down/lights come up. **Sensory clothes/wheelchair wrapping – sensory snakes:** Adapt a piece of clothing or a blanket, or even adapt a wheelchair and add metallic paper and coloured tape, similar to the attachments that Linda's work has. **Hand massage or foot massage:** In my own practice I use these a lot as sensory cue to both start an activity and to end an activity. The massage could be accompanied by music.	**Process:** Case studies that could be a series of images and notes describing the engagement over time; narrative assessment of how and in which way the student engaged.	n/a	Links to SMSC
Informal learning objectives: • To actively explore materials • To make choices and request materials • To work in 2D • To work in 3D	**Rationale:** To use Linda Bell's artwork as a context to support creative exploration. To use the material qualities of her artwork as an impetus for further enquiry. To use her work to promote both sensory and experiential activities and explore materials qualities and the idea of participatory arts and performance in making. **Activities:** The activities here can be very similar to those identified for the – pre-formal learners. Students can engage actively with the sensory aspects. For those students that can actively explore materials, there's opportunities here to combine mark making on paper and glitter that could be added to paint or glue. Paint applied to fabrics such as canvas or calico could be added into the installation. Painted paper could be shredded and explored again and then added to the sensory clouds.	**Process:** Case studies that could be a series of images and notes describing the engagement over time; narrative assessment of how and in which way the student engaged. **Product:** Sensory cloud installation/hangings		Links to SMSC

Curriculum pathways	Entry points to Linda Bell's sculptural works	Notes on process/product/vocabulary and assessment	Vocabulary	Value added
Semi-formal learning objectives: • To respond to the work of an artist • To introduce the concept of an artist • To actively explore materials • To name and request colours, materials, and tools • To use tools appropriately and with intention, i.e., pencil and paintbrushes • To make art/mark making as a response to music • To work in 2D • To work in 3D	**Rationale:** To use Linda Bell's artwork as a context to support creative exploration. To use the material qualities of her artwork as an impetus for further enquiry. To use her work to promote both sensory and experiential activities and explore materials qualities and the idea of participatory arts and performance in making. **Activities:** The activities here can be very similar to those identified for the informal learners with the focus on active engagement within the activities and the promotion of choice making, such as choosing colours or selecting the tools the student would like to work with. **Sensory clouds/hangings:** Making the installations together over time. It could be attached to a pre-made aperture and the students could add their woven element/sensory element each week to see it develop over time. ★ You could also introduce the idea of recycling and how these sculptures can bring focus to wider issues of environmentalism. The use of plastics could make direct reference to plastic waste in the sea. The sculpture could then be disassembled and recycled as part of the learning journey. **Photography:** Students could also timeline the installation by taking photos of the sculpture as it unfolds. **Adding/adapting clothing:** As with the pre-formal entry point, you could introduce the idea of clothes that could be added to/adapted to attaching materials and adding paint etc.	**Process:** Case studies that could be a series of images and notes describing the engagement over time; narrative assessment of how and in which way the student engaged. **Product:** The sculpture itself as a 'product'.	**Communication via communication aids for requesting and choice making** Art Artist Colours Colouring Drawing Fabric Gluing Painting Ribbon	Links to SMSC
Formal learning objectives: • To make work as a response to an artist • To have some biographical understanding of the artist and their work • To work in 2D • To work in 3D • To produce work following a process • To produce work that is immediate • To use art-specific terminology	**Rationale:** To use Linda Bell's artwork as a context to support creative exploration. To use the material qualities of her artwork as an impetus for further enquiry. To use her work to promote both sensory and experiential activities and explore materials qualities and the idea of participatory arts and performance in making. **Activities:** The activities here can be very similar to those identified for the semi-formal learners with the focus on active engagement and choice making. There will be a focus on developing their work through a process and building on skills and knowledge and making links between their work and the work of Linda Bell. **Sensory clouds/hangings:** These could again be documented and models made to develop their ideas. They could look more at how they might attach their weaving and research the qualities of different materials. **Photography:** Students could also timeline the installation by taking photos of the sculpture as it unfolds, or they could document this as drawings or paintings. **Issues-based art, recycling, and environmentalism:** The issue of recycling as outlined in the semi-formal entry point could be documented – making, assembling, and showing the piece and then disassembling and recycling the installation.	**Process:** Case studies that could be a series of images and notes describing the engagement over time; narrative assessment of how and in which way the student engaged. **Product:** The sculpture itself as a 'product'.	Art Artist Batik fabric Colours Colouring Collage Constructing Drawing Fabric Identity Painting Sculpture	Links to SMSC

Assessment

Inclusive assessment

The term assessment comes from the Latin *assidere* which means 'to sit beside'. In an educational context this is the process of observing learning, describing, collecting, recording, scoring, and interpreting information about a student's or one's own learning. There are many ways in which assessment can be inclusive, although it would be qualitative assessment and not quantitative. Assessment would be descriptive in nature and describe the learning, and it would be pertinent to the student.

Ipsative assessment

The term ipsative comes from the Latin *ipse* meaning 'of the self'. In education this means measuring the progress against a student's previous performance. The theoretical basis of ipsative can also be found in humanistic education that sits within an inclusive paradigm, i.e., it focuses on empathy and student interests and is highly personalised. This type of education is oppositional to positivist/behaviourist assessments that focus on quantitative modes of assessment and competency-based assessments.

Example of descriptive/narrative assessment

The following is an example of assessment for a student who would be accessing the semi-formal/formal curriculum model.

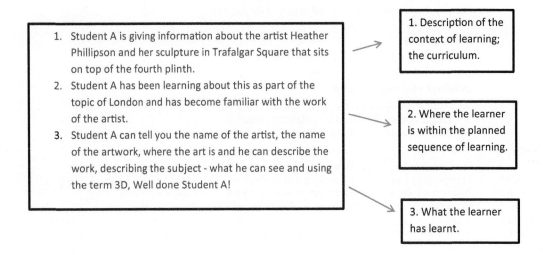

Arts Award

Arts Award is a useful qualification and is structurally inclusive; it is designed to measure individual progress and isn't time bound. The evidence can be collected in a range of formats and is accessible to students who are nonverbal, or less confident in communication, as they can be supported in achieving the award. The structure is less formal and encompasses a wide range of art forms.

Assessment for non-subject-specific learning

The engagement model is a statutory model for describing progress for those learners who are not accessing subject-specific learning. It describes the five areas of engagement as:

- Exploration
- Realisation
- Anticipation
- Persistence
- Initiation

Each of the five areas are interrelated and should be used when assessing pupils who are not engaged in subject-specific study.

How to write about non-subject-specific learning

To evaluate the lateral progression of the learner, I write a description of what they are doing and how that has changed in a very descriptive fashion and how it relates to their specific baseline (ipsative assessment). I then examine and reflect on the writing. Using the appropriate word(s) from the earlier list of five areas is helpful for describing engagement and also becoming more confident in doing so.

Case studies

Case studies are always useful for capturing qualitative assessment. This is explored in more detail in chapter 10.

Concluding notes

Contemporary art supports an inclusive approach to pedagogy (see also chapter 8 on anti-ableist pedagogy). This chapter and the previous one both offer entry points to creative exploration and outline approaches to inclusive assessment. Creativity and the opportunities to explore and define it within an inclusive pedagogy are figured in both chapters. This is further explored in chapter 11, which uses creativity as a device to make the paintings of Frans Hals meaningful and accessible. Creativity and inclusion and the ability to reconfigure, reorganise, and see new possibilities are also touched upon in chapter 12, which explores relaxed performances with interviews from Jess Thom of Touretteshero and the English National Opera.

Artists for further enquiry

The following table is based on a resource that was developed jointly by Dr Sandra Hiett of Liverpool Hope University and Lauren Stichter, Director of Art Education, Moore College of Art & Design, Philadelphia. The resource was shared at the NSEAD special interest group on anti-ableist pedagogy.

Artists	Practice
Aaron McPeake Aaron McPeake is a visually impaired artist. In his PhD thesis, *Nibbling at Clouds: The Visual Artist Encounters Adventitious Blindness,* he explores the impact of vision loss on the visual artist, considering his own practice and other artists who experienced sight loss.	Aaron works predominantly with sculpture that can be interacted with and explored. His work investigates a range of narratives, including personal narratives. Aaron also explores sound and touch to enhance the experiences and readings of his work. His practice also covers film, installation, photographs, and paintings. He likes to explore numerous readings of his work based on the viewers' interactions with the pieces. **More information can be found at**: www.aaronmcpeake.com
Adam Reynolds (1959–2005) Adam was a sculptor, curator, and teacher. He was influential in the disability arts movement, serving on the Board of Shape Arts both as a Trustee (1986–2005) and Chair (1990–1997). The Adam Reynolds Memorial Bursary was set up at Shape Arts in 2007 after his untimely death in 2005. The bursary provides opportunities for disabled artists to develop their work.	Working with lead, copper, steel, and glass, Adam's desire was to 'express apparent contradictions and to help others enjoy the contradictory nature of the universe'. This was apparent in his lead series exploration with a lead balloon and kite. Adam said of being disabled: 'I am clear that my greatest strengths stem from the fact of being born with muscular dystrophy, apparently my greatest weakness'. Adam mainly used scrap materials and found objects, making his viewers question the value and beauty of these. This was 'founded on my lifelong experience of disability and the desire to challenge the commonplace assumption that this renders life all but useless and without value'. **More information can be found at**: www.shapearts.org.uk/Pages/News/Category/adam-reynolds-award
Faith Bebbington 'My . . . practice stems from having cerebral palsy, a disability that is almost imperceptible to most people, but has a big impact on my daily life. As a child wearing calipers, having my leg in plaster for months . . . made me particularly conscious of my own and other people's physical movements'. (Taken from the press release of The Figure: An Exploration of the Human Body in Motion, January 2017 at dot-art Gallery.)	'My artistic practice initially stemmed from having cerebral palsy, a disability that has made me curious about how people and animals move. I explore this through figurative sculptures playing with balance, the process of falling, and capturing sequences of movement whether human or animal'. (Taken from https://faithbebbington.co.uk/) **More information can be found at**: https://faithbebbington.co.uk/
Jade Ramos This fine arts major who is minoring in textiles has less than 10% of her vision and uses layers and textures to spread messages about disability rights and to spotlight artists who made fabulous art with visual impairment.	'My thesis is me "writing" paintings made by artists who had visual impairments that no one talks about, like Rembrandt, Claude Monet, Edgar Degas, Georgia O'Keeffe,' she said. And: 'O'Keeffe had tunnel vision, that's why she painted all those really zoomed-in images of flowers'. (Taken from www.moore.edu/news/jade-ramos-artist-and-disability-activist) **More information can be found at**: www.instagram.com/oneojo/

Artists	Practice
Judith Scott 'No object was out-of-bounds. . . . She became more and more focused and would not allow interruption or distraction. She also became more discerning in her selection of threads and yarns, considering various hues and shades, wrapping the treasure she had gathered until she alone decided a piece was complete'. (Taken from www.textileartist.org/textile-artist-judith-scott-uncovering-innate-talent)	Wrapping and fibre art, wrapping a range of objects in threads to make cocoon-like sculptures. 'Her process was erratic and instinctive. She would wrap thread and yarn around anything she could get her hands on; she appropriated magazines, chairs and even a bicycle wheel'. (Taken from www.textileartist.org/textile-artist-judith-scott-uncovering-innate-talent) **More information can be found at**: www.textileartist.org/textile-artist-judith-scott-uncovering-innate-talent
Rebecca Horn Rebecca Horn explores the physicality of objects, creating objects that directly relate to the human experience. Her art is informed by her illness that she experienced as a child and her childhood in post-war Germany.	She explores the idea of the externalised object, working with the body and extending it and making direct links with the body and body modification and the external/internal. These pieces work as both sculptures and as part of performances too. Her work explores anxiety and depression and the human connection. She uses her work to reduce 'loneliness by dealing with bodily forms'. Rebecca reveals that her working practices allow her to bring balance. She also uses music and musical instruments in her work, asking the viewer to listen and experience rather than to interrogate the piece and look for meaning. There are also historical references within her work that explore broader themes of historical amnesia, particularly in reference to war. **More information can be found at**: www.rebecca-horn.de
Riva Lehrer Riva Lehrer is an artist, writer, and curator who focuses on the socially challenged body. She is best known for representations of people whose physical embodiment, sexuality, or gender identity have long been stigmatized. (Taken from www.saic.edu/academics/departments/low-residency/events/visiting-artist-riva-lehrer)	Riva Lehrer was born with spina bifida and throughout her life has undergone surgery because of this. Her work explores issues of physical identity with a particular focus on disability and how this is culturally depicted. **More information can be found at**: www.rivalehrerart.com
Susan Dupor 'As an artist who is Deaf, I am constantly exploring my identity as a Deaf woman. . . . There were moments when I vented my emotions, and others when I wanted to celebrate the uniqueness of Deaf culture and seek the ironies of being Deaf in a hearing world'. (Taken from www.deaf-art.org/profiles/susan-dupor)	Susan works as a painter exploring Deaf culture and her lived experience as a Deaf woman. **More information can be found at**: www.deaf-art.org/profiles/susan-dupor
Tony Heaton 'Once people understand disability from the point of view of barriers and exclusion – that is, the Social Model of Disability – they can effect change'. (Taken from www.tonyheaton.co.uk/consultancy.html)	'I am concerned with my own existence and my interaction with both the material and non-material world. In my interaction with other humans, I am almost always reminded that I am perceived as a disabled person, this is manifest in their actions towards me and their interaction with me'. (Taken from www.artsandheritage.org.uk/proposals/tony-heaton-the-grand-tour-with-the-tourettes) 'Much of my work explores my personal analysis of these everyday interactions. Sometimes art making becomes self-psychoanalysis'. (Taken from http://www.tonyheaton.co.uk/statement.html) **More information can be found at**: www.tonyheaton.co.uk

Reference

Chatterjee, H. (2008) *Touch in Museums*. London: Jessica Kingsley Publishers. National Curriculum in England, 2014.

10 Cultural inclusion – developing meaningful partnerships between schools and cultural organisations

The West London Inclusive Arts Festival

How to use this chapter

This chapter outlines the practical and logistical approaches to coordinating an inclusive arts festival. It looks at how practical steps can support the idea of inclusion, how you can embed inclusive principles into both the development and the delivery of a festival, and how you can use these events to increase inclusion and inclusive practices across all partners and spaces. The chapter explores this within the context of the West London Inclusive Arts Festival, outlining some of the steps and stages of the festival from conception through to delivery and evaluation. Throughout the chapter practical examples support this, and a checklist is provided at the end of the chapter.

Interview with an adviser to John Lyon's Charity

The chapter includes an interview with Jean Carter, an adviser to John Lyon's Charity which funds the festival, who discusses their strategic funding in this space and draws out key points.

Background

The West London Inclusive Arts Festival was initially a partnership between two special schools and two cultural partners and funded by John Lyon's Charity. The festival grew to four special schools and two cultural partners and now has six special schools working with six cultural partners and continues to be funded by John Lyons Charity.

The festival places inclusion centrally within the festival structures and uses this to inform all decisions, approaches, and structures. I was in the privileged position of conceiving, developing, and running the festival from its inception and until recently coordinated the festival. This experience has allowed me to understand some of these key principles of an inclusive festival and how to embed them within its structures.

Funding

Case for support, making the case for funding

This is central to why you want to deliver a festival. A case for support helps you to articulate what the intention is and what the impact will be (this may change/shift based on the knowledge that becomes clear through the process of delivery and evaluation). One of the most useful purposes of a case for support is that your key messaging becomes clear as you identify the core purpose and principles of the festival. It also helps you to fully understand the 'shape' of your project so that you can effectively share this with others.

Key headings in a case for support

1. **Who you are**: background information, location, description of the population, and any characteristics that describe your current context
2. **The need**: what is it that you would like to do, why? How does this relate to your current context?
3. **The vision/mission**: articulate the project, describing what would the festival look like; this can be your mission statement
4. **The benefit**: what would you like to achieve, what would be the change/benefit?
5. **Description of partners**: who else would be involved, who are they? Why them? What skills do they have? Do you have a historical relationship, an understanding of each other and how you can work for collective change?
6. **Timeline**: when will it start, how often and where?
7. **Costs**: how much will it cost? Make sure that you include all planning time as a cost

---

DOI: 10.4324/9781003122258-10

8. **Evaluations**: how will you evaluate the project?
9. **Legacy/future plans – where next?**

And remember

- Think about your audience. If you use acronyms, spell them out the first time that you use them
- Use bullet points to summarise information
- Use data/evidence to support your case
- **Tip: You can use this as a checklist to support you with developing your case for support and your vision. I would suggest using PowerPoint and use each bullet point as a heading to elaborate on.**

Build momentum

Share and present your case for support. You will need consensus and buy-in from across your organisation and a shared common language and understanding for all those involved. Make this an explicit part of your project. Organise meetings, share and take views and adapt. This will mean that you will have a robust case for support that will have the greatest impact for all involved.

Tip: financial contingency

When looking at your costs, add either 5% or 10% for contingency funding. This will allow you 'flex' if you encounter any additional unforeseen costs and can also help you develop/expand areas of the project that have potential for further growth.

Tip: link to the school development plan and Artsmark accreditation

Look at how the festival or project can support wider school areas of development. Festivals and projects involving collaboration, co-production, and joint working can be great vehicles for driving institutional change, both within schools and with cultural partners. Signpost and acknowledge these as part of the impact. If the project/festival is linked to a school development plan, you can also use this to gain accreditation for the Artsmark award. This ties directly into how the project will deliver change through measurable impact.

★ Artsmark is the only creative quality standard for schools and education settings, accredited by Arts Council England.

Timelines and communications

Fundamental to any success and particularly important when working with a wide range of partners and stakeholders is a communication strategy. Schedule your communications and consider their purpose within the overarching structure of the project – how do they support/impact on the project development and progress? Make sure that this also contains when all key pieces of information should be shared, and key actions undertaken.

Consider the function of meetings and be explicit about the aims – what is it that you want to achieve? How do they support the overall structure and delivery of the festival/project? When chairing these meetings, ensure inclusion is part of the structure and that there is equity in voices; introduce everyone and their role and outline the intentions of the meeting. Some organisations do not formally start meeting until all participants have spoken. These meetings are great opportunities to develop rapport and build shared common purpose, to unlock potential and increase the impact and the reach of the project. I would strongly recommend bullet pointing your minutes and actions and who owns that action, as it will help with organisation and moving things forward. Remember that within a communication strategy not all communications need to be formalised; some can be catch-ups, allowing you to build rapport, increase impact, and reduce paperwork.

A festival on a mission

To this end we aimed to develop long-term relationships that work across all these spaces. Under the auspices of the West London Inclusive Arts Festival, through consultation and dialogue we developed a sustainable network that will deliver fundamental and long-lasting change throughout the festival and beyond (legacy). Consider legacy as an integral aspect of your festival's design.

Inclusive structures

These structures were consciously embedded and overtly signposted within the structure of the festival so that all found the festival an empowering process, and co-production supported this. See chapter 2 on what inclusion looks like for more information on co-production.

Top tip

Consider access to themes and plan multiple entry points to include all students. See chapter 9 on contemporary art and inclusive pedagogies that explores contemporary art and maps entry points into this in relation to various curriculum pathways.

Festival design: planning entry points into a multifaceted festival

The festival's driver was to promote inclusion and inclusive practices and pedagogy across a number of spaces and institutions, specifically within our cultural partners and school partners. This would be realised by developing and delivering a multifaceted festival that met the needs of a wide range of participants at both our partner schools and our cultural partners' venues that included staff, students, and families.

One theme, multiple entry points and events

A collective theme was developed through a planning day where all partners attended. One of our partners, the Wallace Collection, hosted the planning meeting. The venue is situated within a historic building in central London and can be described as both a museum and a gallery. The Wallace Collection has a veritable jewellery box of both images and artefacts that could be mined for inspiration and further enquiry. A brainstorming session was facilitated in the session and numerous entry points into their collection were identified. Over a period of time, a consensus was reached on a title that was broad enough and allowed for a range of entry points for each individual school within the partnership. Through this process the theme developed had enough scope so that all schools within the partnership could meaningfully access it. It was also made clear that they could interpret the theme in the most appropriate and meaningful way for their students.

Top tip

Structural inclusion: all those involved in the delivery should be included in the planning stages. Including everyone ensures that there a diversity of viewpoints and a richer understanding. It increases the chances of impact and creativity and supports the idea of a community with a shared common endeavour.

    In terms of festival design, the diversity of entry points supported the inclusive design of the festival.

    The following are some examples of these entry points:

1. Installation to meet the needs of pre-formal learners/PMLD population. The installation was made of several large wooden framed cubes that students would transition through that had various sensory and experiential activities within them
2. A sensory story, a space, or several spaces that had an overarching simple narrative that was told through sensory and experiential activities. These were supported by independent active engagement and also guided by characters/actors who supported the narrative and the student's engagement
3. Experiencing a movement/dance workshop that directly relates to the overarching narrative/theme
4. A series of art workshops where the process is valued, and the product/outcome was reimagined into the installations and used in the sensory story and other events. For example, using the canvas that was painted by the PMLD learners – they used their feet to make marks, and this was used/reimagined within the installation
5. Making images and artefacts that directly relate to the theme
6. Performing/acting in a play that directly relates to the theme
7. Performing a dance routine that directly relates to the narrative/theme
8. Employing arts facilitators such as potters and animators that can support a range of entry points to the theme

---

Brokering partnerships; roles and responsibilities

In any relationship it is good to be clear about roles so that everyone has a clear understanding of how they can work effectively together. It might mean giving time to this so that there is both clarity about roles but also understanding of unique circumstances.

A central tenet of inclusion is relationships and those relationships defining inclusion in the way in which they interact and work together. Within your objectives developing rapport should be central. This will not only increase the likelihood of a successful partnership but also help to develop a relationship that can continue to reap rewards and benefits going forward and support the legacy of the project. It's worth noting here that if you are working with an external partner, it would be good to dedicate time to developing an understanding of their specific situation, so you can see where there are areas of commonality and shared purpose. This will help you to maximise impact and support each other's areas of development moving forward. In the case of the West London Inclusive Arts Festival, it was supporting our cultural partners' understanding of inclusion and inclusive practice. We worked with our partners in capturing these practices so that each partner had an understanding of what they wanted to achieve through the partnership working. Depending on the duration of a partnership these can be categorised as short term, medium term and long term. An example of this can be seen at the end of the chapter.

Top tip

Be clear about people's roles and responsibilities and make time to understand each other's needs.

Families program

We realised that the inclusion of families would support our parents to access the cultural partners independently of the schools after the festival, and this was part of our legacy strategy. We wanted to use the festival to promote cultural shifts, and this was also an opportunity for families to support our cultural partners in improving this. Families are directly affected by how access is organised; it is part of their lived experience (embodied knowledge). Their knowledge of this and their insights into how to improve it would support our colleagues in developing their inclusive offer. Part of this approach was the idea of developing sounding boards. Sounding boards are made up of a person or a group of people. Ideas and suggestions are presented and dependent on their opinions and responses; they are modified/changed so that chances of success are improved before being implemented.

Co-constructed programming

This programme was to be co-constructed through workshops with parents' groups across the partnerships. The aim was to deliver both parent-specific activities and a programme of family-focused activities with our cultural partners. We also wanted to use this as an opportunity to outwardly promote the experiences of our families, to make them visible and to promote inclusion. This was an initiative that was supported by Portraits of Grit, which is profiled in the family's chapter (Chapter 5).

Parents' steering groups

As mentioned earlier, co-production is an essential element within an inclusive structure, and a steering group is a good way of supporting the development of any project that hopes to increase inclusion in a broad and holistic fashion.

Introducing a steering group

Initially it is worth outlining, in an informal setting accompanied with tea, coffee, and biscuits, what a steering group is and what its function is within the structure of the festival. These events not only help to shape parts of the programming, but they also help to build rapport and long-term relationships that benefit students and the whole school community. Introduce the purpose and function of a steering group and some preliminary ideas so that parents can comment and make suggestions on these. Make it overt that their input will help to shape these events and that their contribution is important and valued. Time needs to be dedicated so that parents are confident in the project, what it is, what it could look like, and how this supports inclusion.

Top tip

Develop a family's sounding board to inform programming and increase impact.

Travel, parking, and access

One aspect that needs to be considered with any large venture, be that with trips out or in the case of a festival with a large number of people accessing a venue, is the consideration of an access plan to that venue. All school outings are risk assessed and inclusive of travel. However, from my experience developing a plan that can address parking and the logistics of public transport is a fundamental part of an inclusive offer.

Developing an inclusive access plan

Transport and access were a common theme identified as an issue in a number of conversations and can significantly detract from a cultural experience if not considered.

The following sections can help you in mitigating this.

Designated parking

Cultural organisations should either have designated onsite parking for minibuses/cars or work in collaboration with the local council/local business to have spaces designated that provide easy access to the venue, i.e., reasonable walking distance when pushing a wheelchair with only a minimum of road crossings. This can also be signposted in an accessible fashion on the website or as part of a communications strategy.

Identifying the closest transport hubs

There should be a map that clearly highlights the closest tube/train/bus stops with a map of how you can then access the venue; again, this should be integral to the communications strategy and website.

Website information

This information should be easily accessible on the organisation's website. The way that information is organised on a website has been identified as a very common barrier to inclusion. When information is hard to find, the 'labour' is passed onto the visitor who then has an additional barrier to face.

Top tip

Develop an inclusive access plan.

CPD opportunities: how to organise them

Continual professional development (CPD) can be transformational in teaching practice and supports teachers in continually developing their practice through sharing their experiences and insights.

These events give teachers the opportunity to present an area of their practice with specific examples and to share the learning and implications. When CPD events are well curated, they not only can support practice, but they also can help to build networks that again can increase impact within this space of arts, culture, and inclusion.

We delivered a dedicated CPD event that signposts best practice in arts, culture, and inclusion, creating a space where cross-sector organisations can meet and engage in professional conversations that inform and support inclusion and help to build future relationships.

During the West London Inclusive Arts Festival, we held the CPD event at the Lyric Theatre in Hammersmith (one of the cultural partners in the festival). The event was entitled *Inclusion in Action in Art and Culture*.

The event is described as follows:
I don't think focus is needed as it's the only heading.

The focus

The focus in on being part of a dynamic CPD workshop with a range of teachers, parents, and cultural organisations. The session will consist of ten-minute presentations that offer insight, knowledge, and experiences within this diverse space. The session will provide the opportunity to share, celebrate, and empower.

Organise your own CPD event

When organising your CPD event consider the following:

1. Rationale: have a statement that articulates the focus and structure of the event
2. Structure: keep it brief, some teach meets have a duration of 2 minutes, however we gave each presenter 10 minutes
3. Have an open call, or reach out to those people that would be interested in presenting/sharing
4. Liaise with all presenters to ensure that the structure works for them and that they are confident and comfortable – build rapport
5. Organise your ticketing using Eventbrite so you can keep a track of numbers
6. If you are including digital presentations, ask that all material is with you before to ensure smooth running of the event
7. Build momentum through networks; ask your partners and presenters to promote; use Twitter if you have a Twitter account and hashtags such as #inclusion #culturalinclusion #teachmeet
8. Have fun!

Measuring impact: case studies and questionnaires

As mentioned earlier, qualitative, descriptive assessment is an inclusive approach to assessment. Case studies are a useful assessment tool that aligns with this. Case studies allow you to use descriptive assessment to tell the story of a student's learning and engagement. Case studies can be tailored to the individual students and therefore are very student specific, capturing their experience and learning over a period of time, or they can focus on a singular event.

Case studies: an inclusive assessment tool

The diversity in which a case study can be used to capture information across a number of students demonstrates its inclusivity as an assessment tool.

Evidence

The evidence used within a case study can be wide ranging and can include anecdotal writing, photographs, and short films. A broad evidence base is better at creating a more multifaceted and richer picture of the student's experience. The case studies that we used during the festival allowed us to collect evidence of the impact for learners as diverse as those accessing a formal curriculum through to those learners accessing a pre-formal curriculum. The next stage involved identifying a specific event or series of events, and evidence was collected that could then be examined and reflected on later.

In one of the instances examined we produced a case study on a student with a diagnosis of autistic spectrum condition who was accessing the formal curriculum. The case study examined a series of creative art lessons and had a specific focus on drama. In these sessions the student developed an understanding of the character he was portraying; he was rehearsing lines and actions and becoming increasingly confident in his empathy and understanding of the character's motivations. This was evident in how his portrayal became steadily more sophisticated and imbued with emotion from the delivery of his lines through to the way he held his body and gestured.

We also used this approach with a pre-formal learner exploring a very specific event, a sensory story. We were able to capture the student's responses and affects to stimuli in the moment, and for this specific learner it denoted a notion of progress through engagement.

Structure of a case study

A description and a rationale

A biographical description of the student observed:

*   Age
*   Sex
*   Descriptions of the learner's disability/barrier to learning
*   How and in what way they learn and how this is supported

Baseline description

This is a qualitative description of how the student presents in the class during activities and can help to describe how and in what they engage. It is good to write this in a narrative, storytelling manner and share with all those familiar with the student for moderation. This process helps to ensure it is a fair description of the learner. The purposes of the baseline are to establish an agreed description of the learner. This moderated description is the baseline to which you can refer when describing the engagement/progress of the learner. This again chimes with ipsative assessment. The progress, both linear and lateral, is described in relation to the student's engagement and progress as opposed to any externalised assessment criteria.

Frequency

I would recommend that you collect evidence at two to three occasions so that your case study tells a story: a beginning (the baseline), a middle, and an end. This will help to present a story of engagement and/or progress. This is also dependent on the situation on which you are reporting; some case studies will focus on collecting information over time as the learning/change will be cumulative, others will be within a specific activity or event. Tailor your case study to meet the needs of the student you are focusing on.

Presenting your case study

There is no uniform approach, but PowerPoint can be useful in presenting information; it allows you to reference a wide range of evidence within one document.

The instance or event

When examining an instance, it is useful to film or photograph the situation and then reflect and describe the situation, considering how the students are engaging, and in what way they are doing this. If the student is engaged in non-subject-specific learning, it is helpful to use the language that describes their engagement as defined by *The engagement model Guidance for maintained schools, academies (including free schools) and local authorities*. The Standards and Teaching Agency, July 2020.

★ The use of engagement when assessing those learners accessing non-subject-specific learning is a mandatory requirement.

Engagement; describing the learning

As mentioned in the previous chapter, the engagement model has five areas of engagement:

- Exploration
- Realisation
- Anticipation
- Persistence
- Initiation

How to describe learning in a case study

Formal curriculum case study

The following is an example of writing taken from a case study used to evaluate the West London Inclusive Arts Festival. The case study was also used for reporting reasons.

The case studies make explicit reference to enjoyment, enthusiasm, and engagement, as these were the headings used within the funding application. These areas were referred to in a holistic fashion as they are implicitly interlinked:

Engagement: active interaction and responsive; we extended this to include problem solving and investigation
Enjoyment: sustained engagement demonstrating curiosity, persistence, initiation, and anticipation
Enthusiasm: positive effects; sustained engagement and positive indicators and anticipation
★ The following three paragraphs refer to the video footage that we used to inform the case study.

Engagement

Video 1: Using the potter's wheel. Student A responds well to both the material manipulation and investigation and the guidance from the potter in forming a pot. Interestingly here, student A also makes connections to experiences/ideas that are abstract; he describes how the pot reminds him of chimneys from The Simpsons. *It would suggest that this stimulating experience supported the student's abstract thinking. This is also seen over the duration of the films documenting student A in drama rehearsals in which he becomes increasingly confident and responsive; he becomes surer in his expression, he emotes more in his movements, and there is a clear progression in his understanding.*

Enjoyment

Student A demonstrates a level of curiosity, in art he executes and problem solves making a picture frame and logos/motifs that he is attaching to the frame. Student A works with persistence and realises his design. This is mirrored in both his acting and singing. Student A's persistence and anticipation are key components within the development/rehearsals. Student A is also seen physical anticipating his lines, and his body movements and smiling suggest that this is a positive experience.

Enthusiasm

As mentioned previously over the rehearsal stage student A's body and demeanour suggests that he becomes increasingly confident. His sustained engagement and the refinement of his performance supports the view that his enjoyment is increasing as his acting progresses, as seen in his demeanour.

Pre-formal curriculum case study

This case study was different as it captured engagement within a specific event, a sensory story. The progress here was lateral. The language also corresponded with the guidance as mentioned earlier. The case study described the time engaged as well as positive effects.

Positive effects

- Smiling
- Verbalising
- Calm
- Attending

Approach

As with the formal learner we decided to approach the headings – Engagement, Enjoyment, and Enthusiasm – in a holistic fashion where they were implicitly interlinked:

Engagement: Active interaction and responsive
Enjoyment: Sustained engagement demonstrating curiosity, persistence and initiating
Enthusiasm: Positive effects; sustained engagement and positive indicators

Engagement

The images show student B demonstrating engagement during different stages of the sensory story installation. It was particularly noted that student B continued to actively engage with the switches and the microphone. Here student B demonstrates both curiosity and persistence but also initiation with this exploration.

Enjoyment

Student B's enjoyment is clearly identified at different stages of the sensory story. This was particularly noted with his interaction with the microphone and his vocalisation.

Enthusiasm

Transitioning and sustaining engagement for an extended period during the sensory story. The sessions were 45 minutes long and populated by a range of experiences and opportunities. Student B appeared alert, transitioned between activities, and engaged with support. This would suggest that student B was curious and that he had contingency to engage. It can be inferred that the 'new' experience of the sensory story was both pleasurable and facilitated his engagement.

   ★ Some students with SEN can find new experiences problematic.

Student questionnaires

The following is an example of a student's questionnaire. These are useful ways of capturing student voice from the learner's perspective and can give insights into their experiences and how they can inform the development of the festival/activities going forward. The questions were designed to draw out these answers in a structured fashion but allowed the students space to give comment and narrative.

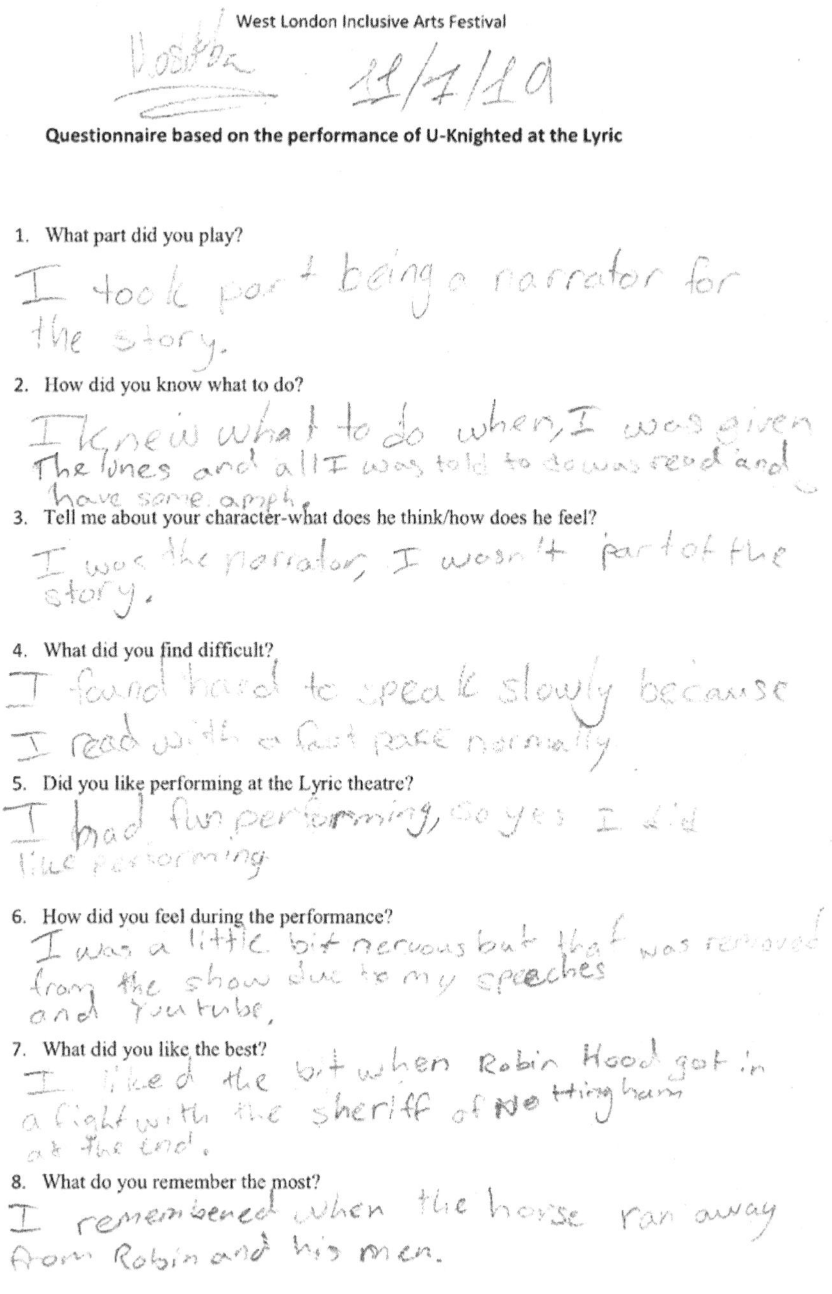

West London Inclusive Arts Festival

Vostok 11/7/19

Questionnaire based on the performance of U-Knighted at the Lyric

1. What part did you play?

I took part being a narrator for the story.

2. How did you know what to do?

I knew what to do when I was given the lines and all I was told to do was read and have some amph.

3. Tell me about your character—what does he think/how does he feel?

I was the narrator, I wasn't part of the story.

4. What did you find difficult?

I found hard to speak slowly because I read with a fast pace normally.

5. Did you like performing at the Lyric theatre?

I had fun performing, so yes I did like performing.

6. How did you feel during the performance?

I was a little bit nervous but that was removed from the show due to my speeches and youtube.

7. What did you like the best?

I liked the bit when Robin Hood got in a fight with the sheriff of Nottingham at the end.

8. What do you remember the most?

I remembered when the horse ran away from Robin and his men.

Image 10.1 Image of a student questionnaire

Guest lists: an ongoing resource

Events and celebrations are great opportunities to engage with your local community, build relationships, and influence in terms of visibility and the inclusion agenda. It is advisable to develop a guest list as an ongoing resource that you can refer to when organising your invitations. It is worth consulting with colleagues so that your guest list captures all those who work and support the school. We also used this as a means to engage with both the local council and our local MP who attended several of the school events. We updated our guest list annually to ensure that all contact information was correct, to remove those who might have moved on, and to include new contacts.

General data protection regulation (GDPR)

Make sure that holding this information is GDPR compliant. Ensure that guests on the list have opted in and have allowed their details to be stored and shared for future events.

Top tip

Develop a guest list and update details annually.

Evaluating partnerships

Integral to the festival is an evaluation process.

The evaluation process encompassed a range of tools, all of which give evidence. Evaluations were then used to tell a narrative/story of the festival to give shape to what happened and describe the impact. They were also used to inform how the festival might develop.

In the following table are the evaluation tools used and their focus:

Evaluation tool	Focus
Student case studies	Student specific and used to tell the story of how and in what way the students accessed the festival and the impact of this. Can be used for a range of learners, from those accessing a pre-formal curriculum through to those accessing a formal curriculum.
Student questionnaires	See example. Semi-structured questions facilitate student voice and describe how and in what ways they accessed the festival and to find out what aspects they found most enjoyable.
Teacher questionnaires	How and in what way they accessed the festival and which aspects they found most and the least useful. How the structure of the festival could be improved and how it supported their professional development.
Cultural partners questionnaires	How and in what way they accessed the festival and which aspects they found the most and the least useful. How the structure of the festival could be improved and how it supported their professional development.
SWOT analysis	SWOT analysis looks at four different aspects: strengths, weaknesses, opportunities, and threats. This analysis was organised as a group activity and as a holistic overview of the festival. It was workshopped and then shared with the group and then additions were made to it. This document directly fed into the structure of the following year's festival.

Budget management: tracking the spend

One easy way of keeping track of budgets, especially if they are large, is to track them on a spreadsheet. If you have a large budget that is broken down into several streams corresponding with different aspects, it allows you to manage them effectively and to add commentary if your spending shifts or changes. These proved hugely useful when reporting on the finances as there were usually a lag in the schools' financial systems and when writing the report to the funder demonstrating that the money was spent well and in line with the funding application.

Increasing inclusion: cultural partners' action plans

We worked with our cultural partners to map the opportunities that the festival presented in helping them develop their understanding and support cultural shifts. These were categorised as short-, medium-, and long-term aims and corresponded to the three years. These aims were to give a sense of direction and trajectory. The table that follows is an example of a short-term aim.

Year 1: short-term aim

These can be described as 'quick wins' and are those things that can be immediately implemented and don't need a period of embedding, or adjustment; however, they do create a culture to support both the medium- and long-term aims. They also are the basis for developing any structures needed for both medium- and long-term changes, for example engaging local parents or teachers in a sounding board/teachers forum.

Year 2: medium-term aim

This is where you start to establish those structures that were introduced in year one and to build on them and where those cultural shifts can start taking place and be articulated. They can become more ambitious and directly impact on areas of programming and reach.

Year 3: long-term aim

Structures continue to be established to promote a cultural shift based on the idea of sustainability and to continually improve inclusion and inclusive practices.

Short-term aims (year 1)	Action needed	Comment
Volunteers to assist/observe during sensory stories alongside specialist teachers – **informal CPD**	Ensure timetabling has embedded training pportunities and that these are signposted	Highlight and value across all parties – inform specialist teachers
Trial of **inclusive access plan** (see the earlier section 'Developing an inclusive access plan')	Start to implement action plan	Could be an indicator of impact/legacy in terms of website and cultural shifts/change
Social stories: videos as part of the access offer – using the festival to drive this resource and co-produce with partner schools	Ensure time is allocated and is part of the contractual agreement with the schools	Inclusion as legacy; improving accessibility via the website
Relaxed performances, are there other types of inclusive performances? Sharing knowledge of these and their principles	Consider the functions/logistics, possibly a tiered approach and pilot these using the festival as driver/context	Make this as an explicit part of the festival and speak with colleagues to co-produce and establish draft principle
Generate conversations with parents/careers/special schools about affordability, access, and engagement with shows – **parent/teacher forum/sounding boards**	Develop a sounding board to work across the partnership	Common theme, collectively most partners want this
Institutional dialogue/professional dialogue	Informal CPD/building rapport and relationships across the partnership; organise partner meetings to facilitate this	Increases capacity of the partnership

Interview with Jean Carter, adviser to John Lyon's Charity

John Lyon's Charity is an influential funder with a strategic approach to working with children and young people including through schools, arts organisations, music hubs, and cultural organisations. It has increased its impact in this space by championing networks and partnership working.

John Lyon's Charity

> John Lyon's Charity gives grants to benefit children and young people up to the age of 25 who live in nine boroughs in North and West London: Barnet, Brent, Camden, Ealing, Hammersmith & Fulham, Harrow, Kensington & Chelsea, and the Cities of London and Westminster. The Charity distributes around £10–12 million in grants each year. The Charity's mission is to promote the life-chances of children and young people through education.
>
> (Taken from John Lyon's Charity website.)

> Since 1991, the Charity has now distributed nearly £200 million to a range of services for young people, including youth clubs, arts projects, counselling initiatives, supplementary schools, parental support schemes, sports programmes, and academic bursaries.
>
> (Taken from John Lyon's Charity website.)

London based, national influence

The geographic area that John Lyon's Charity funds is specific to some London boroughs, and this means that they work with some of the most significant cultural organisations in the UK (that have a national remit). Alongside this national influence, it also influences funders through its publications, conferences, and membership of networks.

Local presence

John Lyon's Charity is also a local funder that listens and responds to need, it brokers relationships and consistently asks the questions: where are the cultural shifts? Where is the legacy?

First-hand experience

Having been one of their grantees, writing both small grant applications and two larger funding applications for the West London Inclusive Arts Festival, I found that I was listened to. John Lyon's Charity considers the voice of the teacher within partnership work as key. I was championed, and the relationship I have with John Lyon's and their team has been transformational. They are a progressive funder who combine their financial strength with their strong commitment to strategic working. This has increased inclusion and inclusive practices within the areas that they fund; they are an ally and an agent for change.

The interview

The interview covers some broad themes from the perspective of a funder. Key points and practical points are drawn out and punctuate the interview. References are made to some of their publications, and these are downloadable from their website.

Jean Carter, adviser John Lyon's Charity

Jean has more than 30 years' experience of working in the space of education, arts, and culture, and has an extensive knowledge of partnership working to maximise impact and reach of inclusion and inclusive practices. Jean has worked on three publications in her role as an adviser to John Lyon's Charity, and these are listed at the end of the interview.

Questions: inclusion and inclusive practices

As the author of the Perspectives publications and as an adviser to John Lyon's Charity:

What do you feel are the most significant barriers to inclusion and inclusive practice within this space and with specific focus on SEND schools and cultural organisations?
What do you feel could mitigate or remove these barriers?

Knowledge

'One of the things that continues to be a barrier in some cases, but I also think has moved on, is the lack of knowledge in organisations of what inclusive practice should be, but I would say that there's more recognition in organisations of where they don't have the skill set, and so recognition of where support is needed'.

Training

'The barrier is actually that there isn't always the knowledge within the organisations to be able to provide relevant inclusion training, and that may have funding implications, so I think a barrier is that more funding may need to be available to support training of the workforce within organisations'.

Willingness

'I would say that there is a willingness from organisations to want to work with schools and teachers who do have the knowledge'.

Solution

'Partnership working can be a solution to barriers'.

Language

[It would be help if there was] 'demystification around what inclusion is, what the language actually refers to, and what it means'.

Shared language and shared understanding

'If you haven't established an agreed understanding of what inclusion is, then it's very difficult to reflect on your own practice to become more inclusive'.

Local knowledge

'[Considerations may include] Are you working with someone who has the local information to be able to deliver and support the project? Do they have the knowledge base to do that?'

Consult with families

'The project needs to be informed by people who know – the parents, families, and carers – the adults who are in a situation where they want access for their family members. We, as professionals, need to be asking them what the access needs are'.

Consult with communities

'Venues, and facilities for the community, need to be informed by the community as to what needs to be in place so that they're accessible'.

Steering groups

'If you have a steering group, working party, or planning group, you may need to consider including family representation and young people who are experiencing the project, where it's appropriate. I've seen inclusive planning groups done very well but you have to put additional thought in, so that it's not lip service'.

DNA

'Equality, diversity, and inclusion should be integral to everything that you do. It then becomes part of the DNA of your organisation'.

Key points

- Identify where you need support and get connected
- Invest in training and seek funding
- Work collectively to reduce barriers
- Develop a shared understanding of language
- Describe inclusion. Where is it in your working?
- Reflect on how inclusive you are
- Local knowledge will help you to understand how you can meet need
- Consult with families and parents
- Consult with the local community
- Meaningfully develop and engage with steering groups
- Make inclusion part of your organisation's DNA

Question: Covid-19

In what way do you think the pandemic has affected the infrastructure that was in place?
  How and in what way do you think this can be addressed?
  What long-term strategic changes do you think need to happen for this to be sustainable?

Blended model

'Some organisations were able to adapt their practice to be online and have now moved to a blended approach in terms of delivery'.

Experience

'People that we're working with have had different experiences'.

Family

'In terms of family engagement, if you look at positives that potentially have come out of the pandemic, [in future] we need to include the family more. It's not just about arts organisations working with the school, its arts organisations working with the young person, through the school and with the school, and including the family, where appropriate'.

Benefit

'What we need to do is to see what has actually been beneficial, and that needs to inform the conversation going forward'.

Online

'It's made organisations think about multiple access points. Online access, for some, is an additional access point'.

Where is the inclusion?

'[Considerations are] How is a blended offer inclusive? In what way? What are the characteristics of the virtual experience that make it inclusive? How can inclusive online access complement other places and spaces?'

Key points

- Consider a blended model
- Consider personal experiences and how these have impacted
- Develop relationships with families to increase reach and impact
- Be inclusive of positive developments and build on these
- Ensure that meaningful online provision is part of the offer
- Consider the characteristics of online and virtual inclusion so that it can be scaled up

---

Question: long-term changes

What do you think is the most significant change that you would like to see in the spaces?

Broader conversations

'One of the positives is that the conversation is broader now, there is more shared learning. I think going back a few years, there was a little bit of fear associated with admitting gaps in knowledge. I think that's changing and it's okay to say we don't know'.

Language

'The importance of language and framing conversations or pieces of work giving prominence and status to such a valuable area'.

Sharing

'Sharing information where there is best practice. I would like to see sharing best practice as much as possible, so that people don't keep going from the standing start. I also think sharing not only when people get it right, but also sharing the challenges. It is important to share when it's not always a success story, but it is part of the learning curve'.

Key points

- Language is central in inclusion, give it status
- Share and attend networks
- Have honest dialogues and share difficulties as well as success

---

Website

www.jlc.london

Key publications

- John Lyon's Charity: Perspectives (2016)
- John Lyon's Change of Perspectives (2019)
- Stand up for SEND (John Lyon's Charity, 2019)

Concluding notes

This chapter explores the principle of inclusion within a festival. It looks at how this was developed both organisationally and structurally, including financially through fundraising to support the festival. The festival was used as a vehicle for change, increasing connections and the school's capacity to promote inclusion and positive change. This collective working chimes with chapter 4 and the importance of creating positive relationships for people with protected characteristics. This is also explored in chapter 6 with the concept of role models and the interview with DJ, a dancer at Corali.

Inclusive arts festival checklist

Structure/document/resource	Purpose in the festival
Case for support	Gives shape and focus and useful for funding applications
Communications strategy and timeline	Supports the strategic development and supports the development of the festival
Co-produced themes	Multiple entry points and diversity of entry points and outcomes are a signifier of inclusion and inclusive practice
Roles and responsibilities	Having clarity on roles and responsibilities helps all to work with a clear purpose
Develop a steering group	This will support the development and delivery of the festival and will support the structural function of the festival
Inclusive access plan	Develop this earlier to reduce and mitigate any tensions that may arise from travel to/from venues
Case studies	Develop and share their structure so that all who are contributing are clear on their function and purpose
CPD event(s)	Develop these early and ensure that they are part of your communication strategy and timeline to allow enough time to build momentum
Guest list	Develop with all partners to ensure reach and that all details are correct
Evaluation/report writing	Ensure that all evaluation tools are shared in good time and are part of your timeline/communication strategy and be clear on what evidence they are providing when writing your report

11 Heritage settings and inclusion; school's partnerships

Through two case studies this chapter explores inclusion and inclusive practices in the heritage sector. The two case studies explore two different approaches to co-production and offer insights into different points of access and to how their collections were made accessible, meaningful, and relevant to students with SEND.

National Trust

The chapter also has an interview with Tiger de Souza MBE, People Engagement Director of The National Trust, in which he discusses his experience of making one of the largest heritage charities in the UK more diverse and inclusive.

How to use this chapter

This book uses both case studies to draw out their practical implication for schools and cultural organisations.

The Maritime Museum case study

The Maritime Museum case study uses a children's book as a way of supporting access and engagement for SEND students and focuses on the initial stages of co-production and the use of simple texts to create connection and enquiry. It looks at how this was used to support a number of entry points and themes and to bridge the two spaces of a museum and a school.

This case study explores the initial stages of the development of a SEND-specific filmed resource developed through a co-production approach.

The Wallace Collection case study

The Wallace Collection explores this through the development of a trip and an outreach session. The case studies look at the ways in which the trip and outreach sessions were co-produced, using paintings from the Wallace Collection to inform a range of activities that made them relevant and accessible to young people with SEND and considering notions of representation and portraiture and inclusion. It looks at the structure of co-production and the points critical to developing meaningful, impactful long-term partnerships.

Both case studies were mapped against current educational policy so that they can be used in schools to demonstrate impact and relevance against these. Key points are distilled throughout the chapter to give practical guidance. At the end of the chapter there are the contact details of the specific SEND approaches that we refer to in the chapter.

The Maritime Museum in Greenwich

The National Maritime Museum (NMM) is a maritime museum in Greenwich, London. It is part of the Royal Museums Greenwich, a network of museums in the Maritime Greenwich World Heritage Site, like other publicly funded national museums in the United Kingdom.

The Wallace Collection

The Wallace Collection is a collection of the fine and decorative arts formed in the eighteenth and nineteenth centuries by four successive marquesses of Hertford and the fourth marquess's heir Sir Richard Wallace. It was left to the British nation in 1897 and opened as a national museum in June 1900 in Hertford House, a grade II listed building in central London. The Wallace Collection is a closed national collection that is both a gallery and a museum.

DOI: 10.4324/9781003122258-11

Case study: the Maritime Museum

Context

The school (Westminster Special Schools) was invited to participate in a daylong workshop to facilitate a SEND-specific filmed resource based on a children's storybook. The storybook was written previously with no direct reference to the Maritime Museum. The project is being supported by Kusuma Trust.

Focus

The focus was to develop two films that support exploration of SEND and enquiry using the story of Immi. Immi is an illustrated children's book that based in the cold regions of the world, telling the story of Immi, a young girl, who over the course of the book fishes through a hole in the ice catching food and colourful objects such as leaves and flowers to decorate her igloo. The objects that she finds make a connection to other places and another child on a tropical beach. The filmed resource would be a way of bridging engagement between schools and the museum. We also discussed that the project would have an overt anti-ableist approach. See chapter 8 on anti-ableism for further information.

Definition of ableism

Ableism describes discriminatory behaviours that favour non-disabled people.

Partnerships negotiated

The protagonists

- Paul, Tanja, Mike, and Estela: Westminster Special Schools
- Ruth Boley: learning team manager
- Dwayne Rose: schools learning producer
- Noel Hayden: SEND specialist
- Karin Littlewood: author and illustrator
- Amanda Saakwa-Mante: pop-up project educational manager
- Chris and Jay: Wolfpack Film productions

The author and the book

The author and illustrator of the book is Karin Littlewood. The author discussed her practice and outlined the book and the key themes of colour and connectedness. The book has been used on many occasions in schools to support literacy and explore a wide range of contemporary themes. The book is very visual and sequentially tells how Immi collects objects with colours increasing as the story unfolds.

Image 11.1 Image of the front cover of *Immi*
Source: © Karin Littlewood

Hidden histories

Westminster Special Schools, my home school, is located in central London and has a high proportion of students from ethnic minorities. The idea of using a book where the main character is female, non-white, and non-European appealed to the school. This allowed space for other narratives to be told, and the notion of a global, multicultural perspective is one that we positively promote within the school. The notion of global citizenship and the two characters, one in the heat of a tropical beach and the other in the cold regions of the world, illustrate that we may live in different places, but we are connected. The idea of connection and the notion of friendship is one that all schools support through their teaching practices. This also resonates with the protected characteristics and equality duty as explored in chapter 4 on policy and strategy.

A connection to a museum

A specific part of the museum's collection was identified: the Pacific Encounters Gallery and the images and artefacts that are found there. The story was positioned as an entry point to the museum via this specific gallery, and some of the video resources would be filmed in the space. Artefacts from the gallery were used to inform the discussion and questions were posed: how might they be used to support the learning intentions of the project? How might they be introduced in a classroom setting? The story and the accompanying video were couched as an entry point to visiting the museum, a means to engage in a meaningful activity prior to visiting and seeing/experiencing these activities within the museum.

Schools' partnership: roles and values, how to maximise impact?

Getting to know you

The schools talked about their specific populations and their needs so we could get to know and understand the schools, and they described their curriculum models. We discussed how this knowledge could be used.

- Mapping against curriculum pathways; pre-formal, informal, semi-formal and formal (see the following four sections for definitions)
- Mapping SMSC (social, moral, spiritual, and cultural development)
- Mapping cultural capital

Pre-formal curriculum

This is the pathway for learners who have profound and multiple learning difficulties (PMLD). Students are mostly wheelchair users, have physical disabilities and complex medical needs, and have profound developmental delay. The learners here make profoundly slow progress, and the learning is often through sensory and/or experiential activities. Learning is often improvised and is based on the students' affectations and responses to stimuli and historical knowledge of these (pupil centred). All communication is nonverbal, and knowledge of the learner is essential for meaningful activities to be offered. Progress may be lateral and static in nature with a focus on quality of experience.

Informal curriculum

The informal curriculum is focused on active exploration and works within a play-based paradigm where students are 'learning to be, rather than learning to do'. The curriculum will have lots of sensory activities that facilitate active engagement and communication, expressing needs and wants, and may have learners that are both verbal with limited language and nonverbal. The curriculum, like that of the pre-formal, is tailored to the needs of the learner (pupil centred); progression will often be lateral in nature and the focus will be on generalising learning through rehearsal and repetition. Students will require visual supports and communication aides.

Semi-formal curriculum

The semi-formal has aspects of the informal such as sensory and exploratory, but learners will make linear progress, although the rate of progression will be slow. The generalisation will be supported through rehearsal and repetition. There might be more progress in the acquisition of skills, rather than knowledge. Again, students will require visual supports and communication aides.

Formal

Learning over time is subject specific and the progress is linear in nature and faster. Students may require visual supports and communication aides.

To effectively co-produce a resource, it is important that you

- Understand the school, its young people, and their needs
- Describe current curriculum needs/developments, as they will likely be pertinent to other schools
- Describe the curriculum model and explain specific terminology to ensure understanding
- Frame your conversation in wider education policy so that schools will be able to articulate the full potential/impact of the project

SMSC, as defined by Ofsted

Spiritual

Explore beliefs and experience; respect faiths, feelings, and values; enjoy learning about oneself, others, and the surrounding world; use imagination and creativity; reflect.

Moral

Recognise right and wrong; respect the law; understand consequences; investigate moral and ethical issues; offer reasoned views.

Social

Use a range of social skills; participate in the local community; appreciate diverse viewpoints; participate, volunteer, and cooperate; resolve conflict; engage with the 'British Values': democracy, the rule of law, liberty, and respect and tolerance.

Cultural

Appreciate cultural influences; appreciate the role of Britain's parliamentary system; participate in cultural opportunities; understand, accept, respect, and celebrate diversity.

Co-production: activities that could accompany the videos

The schools were also asked to suggest some activities that would support their students in accessing the book to inform some of the activities that would be filmed.

Maritime Museum's pre-existing SEND resources: Sensory Seas

This was presented to the group with the idea of building on these and adding to this resource. The resources could be linked or extend and enhance the students' experiences. Noel Hayden delivered a presentation of **Sensory Seas**, a journey told through objects and actions and a call-and-response activity (a statement quickly followed by an answering statement) which was based on sea shanties and other sensory activities. We explored the narrative and the principles that underpinned its development and the entry points of engagement for students.

Principles of a sensory story

Sensory stories are short stories with simple text. The story is told through sensory activities and experiences that support meaningful engagement. Sensory stories are particularly beneficial for students with sensory processing disorders (SPD), profound and multiple learning difficulties (PMLD), autism spectrum condition (ASC), and other special educational needs and disabilities (SEND).

Handling objects from the museum's collection

We were also given the opportunity to handle objects from the museum's collection that related to the Pacific Encounters Gallery to see what responses they elicited. These were explored through touch; we also considered their uses so that they might inform our thinking in terms of the project and resources that could complement this.

Stick chart

One of the objects explored was a stick chart. These stick charts were used in the Marshal Islands by the Marshallese to navigate the Pacific Ocean by canoe. The chart represents ocean swells and the islands. This object is beautiful and practical in its use as a recording device to aide journeys and suggests an object that could 'map and capture the learning journey'. It could grow, and it shows the changes within the story's narrative over time – the changes in colour and connection and other story objects – and chimed with the idea of weekly exploring/weekly explorers etc. The objects and images attached could be used to support the student's recall of the story.

Handling objects to support learning

- Be creative in how you can use objects to support learning
- Consider how an object might be used to support a story and how the object itself will change and grow as the story progresses
- Objects can be great for students to make connections and anticipate learning and can create a sense of occasion
- Objects of reference can support young people in anticipating learning/activities as a communication device

---

Entry points to the story of Immi

The following table presents some entry points that were discussed in relation to the book and linked to various curriculum pathways. I would like to acknowledge the contributions of my fellow teachers in developing them.

These are general entry points that can be developed further.

Activity	Link to story	Curriculum pathway
Transparent umbrella • Where the snow could fall from, it could also mirror the igloo. The decorations such as feathers, leaves etc. that are made over the course of the story could also be attached here.	Igloo/snow	• Pre-formal • Informal • Semi-formal ★ Could be used as part of a sensory story
Sensory igloo • Create a space to tell stories in, maybe a tent? Using sensory lights iridescent fabrics etc.	Igloo	• All curriculum pathways
Sensory/spicy birds • Using a bird shape and sticking different spices and add different colours to build a collection of them over time. They can be used to support memory and be revisited and used to identify colours or used in colour matching activities. The birds could also be hung and used as decorations.	Bird decorations	• Semi-formal
Feather activities • Matching coloured feathers to the same-coloured square/straw etc. • Sensory painting, making a feather drawing using handprints. Cutting these out after they have dried. • Collaging photocopies of feathers • Mark making on to feather templates • Colour mixing/cause and effect on to feather templates	Feather decorations	• Informal • Semi-formal • Formal
Playdough flowers • Make playdough flowers and add essences	Flower decorations	• Informal • Semi-formal
Leaf activities • Stamping onto leaves using different shaped stamps • Collecting leaves • Pressing leaves into clay	Leaf decorations	• Semi-formal • Formal

Activity	Link to story	Curriculum pathway
Colourful flowers • Using white paper flowers and adding colour to them by painting; they can be added using a pipet as a choosing activity and dropping the colours from above	Flower decorations/colour change referenced in the book	• Semi-formal • Formal ⋆ Could be used as an attention autism task
Fishing activity • Ice hole fishing using water or other liquids so that students could feel around and enjoy that sensation as well as perhaps 'catching' different objects placed in the bowl/box	Fishing activity	• Pre-formal
Movement in wheelchairs mirroring currents/sledges • Students could experience a sleigh ride, either in their chairs or on the gym mats, sliding along with fans to mimic the cold arctic wind and sound effects, maybe even some 'snow' falling, or go on a longer ride mimicking an object being carried along by the ocean currents	Sleigh ride/ocean currents	• Pre-formal/PMLD entry point
Sensory trays • Sensory trays (stations) placed around the room/gallery space story telling – referencing the story – characters and the sensory experiences in relation to the story	Whole book	• All curriculum pathways
Edible snow • Actively explore edible snow	Snow	• Informal • Semi-formal
Finding hidden objects in ice • Actively exploring ice to find the hidden decorations	Fishing/decorations	• Informal • Semi-formal
Aurora borealis • Geographic links • Experiential activities using lights/colour change • Craft activity using black sugar paper, glitter, and chalk	Geography/location	• All curriculum pathways

Rationale for the video resources

Video 1: to introduce the author, the story, and the museum

The focus here was to introduce the author, the book, and the museum and to acknowledge their cultural value. This would overtly point to their significance in relation to **cultural capital**; the author, the book, and the museum and signposting the filming would adopt a total communication approach.

Video 2: a range of entry points and activities to support students in accessing the story

The video would be instructional with activities-based small clips, filmed in the gallery to inform teachers of the entry points and how they can support class-based activities. The video would outline the resources needed and refers to SEN-specific pedagogy such as attention autism and lis'n'tel.

Activities would correspond to the various curriculum pathways and have a range of sensory and experiential approaches. Cross-curricular topics where appropriate would be signposted to such as Geography and Personal Social Health Education. Instructions would be broken down, allowing for the pace of the activities to be determined by the class teacher and could support repetition, rehearsal, and over-learning so that students could become secure and confident in their learning and at a pace that is appropriate to them.

The resource used in the activities would use easy-to-find and affordable materials so that this wouldn't be a barrier. Learning objectives would be clear with references to cultural capital and SMSC development.

A total communication approach would also be adopted for this film.

Attention Autism

Attention Autism is a specific approach designed by Gina Davis, a specialist speech and language therapist. The objectives of this specific approach are to develop communication, both spontaneous and natural, through a series of structured, highly motivating activities.

Lis'n'tel

This is a specific approach designed to support communication and understanding. It uses a highly repetitive and rhythmic approach to storytelling with ritualistic gestures.

Total communication environment and approach

Describes all the different ways that we communicate. Using all these approaches maximises the chance of meaningful understanding. These are:

- Eye contact – facial expression
- Body language – vocalisations
- Speech – symbols
- Photos – writing/drawing
- Objects – signs and gestures

Teachers' notes

It was decided that teachers' notes would be developed to elaborate further on the opportunities that these resources presented to the school in terms of evidencing against wider school needs and signposting to them. The notes could act as a jumping-off point for further enquiry and co-production.

Further opportunities

We discussed further opportunities that could support and enhance the resources, and some of these are outlined as follows.

Craft boxes

One idea was to develop craft boxes that could be sent into schools to enhance the connection to the museum and start a 'conversation'. The furthers the notion of connection and the continuation of the story into the gallery spaces, or the onward journey to the sensory seas resource.

Environmentalism

The book could be used as a context to explore the theme of environmentalism and the idea of recycling and the issue of pollution and plastic in the sea, and how we can take positive action to reduce this. Objects in the books that are collected from the sea could be refashioned into 'gifts' or decorations, and then gifted to friends, which also supports the notion of connectedness.

Case study: the Wallace Collection

Frans Hals and The Male Portrait at the Wallace Collection

Context

The idea was to co-produce a project, designing meaningful and appropriate activities that would support a range of students to respond to the Wallace Collection.

The project would be delivered through both students visiting the collection and an outreach session. This is arranged into two case studies offering insights into the process of co-production. The focus of the project was the Frans Hals portraits in the curated exhibition entitled 'Frans Hals: The Male Portrait' with a focus on *The Laughing Cavalier*.

The protagonists

- Paul, Pamela, and Clara: Westminster Special Schools
- Amy Chang: formal learning producer
- Luke Crookes: musician

Background to the exhibition: 'Frans Hals: The Male Portrait'

In autumn 2021, the Wallace Collection celebrated Frans Hals's (1582/3–1666) most famous and beloved painting, *The Laughing Cavalier*, completed in 1624. Since it entered the Wallace Collection in 1865 as the only work by Hals, this iconic image had never previously been seen together with other works by the artist, and it formed the centrepiece of the exhibition.

(Taken from the Wallace Collections website.)

Planning a visit

Description of the students

The group of students who would be visiting the Wallace Collection are all over 16 (aged between 16 and 19) and are accessing a semi-formal curriculum with a focus on a functional/skills-based curriculum.

Planning visit to the museum prior to the trip

The initial stages of co-production

The purpose was to visit the exhibition alongside Amy Chang, the formal learning producer, to identify how and in what way the students would access the exhibition and the Wallace Collection.

Posing questions

We posed several questions around the historical portraits of Frans Hals. How would a culturally diverse group of disabled students meaningfully access the exhibition? We also considered the notion of equity within this relationship.

Identified entry points

- **What is a portrait?** Making a frame at school that can be taken to and added to at the Wallace Collection, using the frame to demarcate a portrait – a transitionary object that is used in both the school and the gallery as a device to frame a portrait
- **Selfies**: taking photos of themselves ('selfies') and bringing them into the Wallace, they could then choose one of the portraits and appropriate this by adding their portrait on top – collaging and making new work. Considering themselves as portraits in the Wallace Collection and representative and inclusive of them
- **Contrasts**: using some of the fabrics seen in the portrait. The paintings are mostly monochrome with contrasting fabrics: black and white, heavy and light fabrics
- **Strike a pose!** Considering posing and using props to support this; dressing up and posing in the gallery.

The students would also be supported by Luke, a musician in the gallery space. Luke has a long-standing relationship with the gallery using an improvised approach to music making to facilitate engagement and creative responses to their collection.

Supporting enquiry through music

Luke had identified the following ways in which he would support this enquiry within the gallery space:

- Being together with the portraits looking, noticing, responding to, and imagining what the portraits have in them
- Improvising and responding with creative ideas, words, and sounds to bring the characters to life
- Becoming the portraits in the gallery space (posing)
- Family portrait/group portraits in the gallery space (posing)
- Creating our own portraits in the gallery space (posing)

Resources developed before the visit

Before a visit takes place, it is appropriate to develop resources that will help the students have some understanding of the trip and the activities in order to reduce anxiety and increase the impact of their learning.

Social story

The social story contained imagery of the journey: where the students were going, whom they would meet, and the activities that they would be participating in. This was predominantly a visual support and sequential, so that it would support the students in understanding the structure of the day and reduce anxiety.

Plan the structure of the day

When planning any trip, it is good to develop an itinerary so that you maximise the learning opportunities and sign-post these to all those who will be supporting the students. You should also consider the practical logistics of toilets, travel, lunch etc. It also means that everyone has a clear understanding of what will be happening, who is leading, and what the intended learning is. This also helps with developing a social story for the students and sequencing the activities to reduce anxiety.

Exploring the paintings in the gallery space

The students had a series of structured activities in the gallery space that encouraged them to look and respond in a physical way. They were asked to look and share what they could see, striking poses and recreating gestures and discussing how the poses made them feel. Students were posed questions and asked to consider what a portrait is for and how you might want to present yourself, for example, powerful, confident etc. Musician Luke supported these responses, capturing moments and facilitating this improvised and performance-based enquiry.

Abstract concepts made accessible

By anchoring abstract concepts such as emotions in concrete activities such as poses, it made them more accessible as a concept for the students to understand in a meaningful way.

Key points

- Consider prior learning and build on this
- Consider a social story to reduce students' anxiety
- Consider an itinerary for the day and share this
- Map entry points to make the visit meaningful and impact

Case study 2: outreach

Description of the students

The group of students who would be accessing the Wallace Collection via an outreach session are all of a mixed age and are accessing a pre-formal curriculum with a focus on sensory and experiential learning.

PMLD outreach session: developing ideas

The planning for the outreach session was similar to that of the over-16 group in that we first identified meaningful entry points to the paintings that would inform the outreach session. They are elaborated on next and demonstrate how these historical portraits were made relevant meaningful and informed a creative enquiry for these students.

PMLD: pre-formal entry points identified through co-production

Structure

The sessions were structured as an initial get to know you, using the pre-planned activities/entry point identified earlier. Marc and Amy planned these sessions within the timetable developed. A professional conversation then took place, looking at students' responses to the activities presented – their voice added to the potency of co-production.

Sense of self: direct reference to the idea and concept of portraiture

We considered the notion of *sense of self* and how this could be facilitated through a sensory experience using materials that refer to the qualities of the painting and specifically the fabrics depicted. We also considered the concept of phenomenology and the idea of being present as well as the idea of subjective experiences, responding to the material explored and experienced that directly refers to the fabrics in the Frans Hals paintings.

Phenomenology

Phenomenology is the study of individuals' lived experience of the world, their subjective experience. By being curious about this and how experiences are subjectively lived, it can help to inform us, or reorient how we view or understand that experience. Presenting materials and the students' experiences and responses to them, of touching, manipulating, and feeling a material, the students' connection to it and how it made them feel is central to this highly personalised pedagogy.

Contrasts within the portraits of Frans Hals

Frans Hals contrasting use of light and dark in his paintings offered another entry point for exploration. Faces could be lit by light, and light could be tracked or contrasted within a space with lights coming up and lights going down. The heavy, dark velvet fabrics and the use of light white lace and how these also contrasted in their sensory qualities was another avenue to consider, how could they be experienced and worn in the process of building towards a portrait of contrasts.

The grand gesture

The group explored the idea of the grand gesture in relation to the bold brushwork of the Frans Hals portraits. In direct references to the idea of the paintbrush, students could experience the texture of a variety of brushes as an activity. These brushes could be explored on their hands and feet prior to a painting activity in a similar fashion to that of TacPac. This sensory exploration of brushes echoed how the paint was applied to the canvas by Frans Hals. Using black paint on white paper, or white paint on black paper, supports the notion of contrast and drama within the artwork.

TacPac

TacPac uses touch and a range of textures alongside music and works on the premise of sensory communication between two people. TacPac is mostly used with students who are accessing a sensory curriculum such as pre-formal or informal curriculum pathways as outlined earlier in the chapter.

A memento

The focus of the workshops is on process, and this is where the value is placed. There could be some very pleasing outcomes as a result of these explorations, however, which could then be reimagined into a piece of art that could be sent home for parents and carers.

Reimagining

This describes work that is produced through a process. The outcome of the process is then reimagined into a product and might be used in displays etc. By clearly labelling this 'process', the value is still placed on the process.

Prior learning, building on experiences

We discussed how aspects of the sensory exploration could take place prior to the outreach session. The Wallace Collection already had some materials that directly referenced the paintings and these could be posted to the school as a means to start a conversation of enquiry with the students prior to the outreach session taking place.

Key points
- Plan, discuss, and build relationships so that all are heard
- Anticipate activities and share information on students
- Develop a working timetable for the day

- Ensure that student voice is heard through co-production and build in **getting to know you** as an objective
- Make time to talk/discuss and share ideas and how they might be realised
- Consider the long term/legacy of the project

Marc Woodhead on the on the importance of co-production

'I have to say the importance of co-production cannot be overstated. If you take an extraordinary work of art like Frans Hals's *Laughing Cavalier,* and really look closely at it with everybody in the room and make this process unscripted and live in the moment, if everybody feels part of this creative process, extraordinary things will happen. Everybody in the room engaged with the particularities of the painting and the uniqueness of each student and their responses. The slowing down, imagining different perceptions of the students, utilising the responses and ideas of all the wonderful learning assistants, creating an environment together where we can play together, amazing things happened through this collaboration'.

The diagram shows how the entry point developed after the initial visit and the student's responses

The diagram offers a sequence; however, this is only a suggestion, and the entry points could be tailored to the needs and interests of each student and informed by them and their responses.

Rationale

During the initial meeting with the students, we had a conversation. In consideration to the student's initial responses (co-construction), we formulated a sequence of entry points as detailed by the following. This is just one idea that has 'flex' and could be adapted to include a painting/crafting/messy exploration activity.

Gilded/decorative frame

This can be used during the activities as point of exploration and used to frame the student that can be photographed, printed, and sent home as a memento.

A bespoke sensory resource: the light lace oversized collar

A physical extension of the painting. The velvet cloke would be a vehicle to experience a variety of sensory entry points into the Frans Hals painting. It would allow for:

- **Wrapping and draping** around students so that they can experience the light texture of lace. This could be accentuated by ribbons that flow and give a sense of lightness, they could be placed on the student or wafted in the air so that they might be tracked and interacted in a dance-like fashion
- **Pockets**: these could be used to contain 'light' smells such as lavender and add to the sensory exploration

  ★ Sequence of exploration: it would be wise to focus on one aspect/sensory pathway at a time so that students don't find it too overwhelming

Image 11.2 Frans Hals *Laughing Cavalier*
Source: © The Wallace Collection

A dance to Frans Hals

Exploring light and dark, quick and slow, mimicking the brushwork in the painting and the concepts of

- Light: quick movements
- Dark: heavier, slower movements

This can be performed listening to baroque music.

Possible sequence of activities

1. Exploration of faces using soft brushes (make-up brushes) of the face – in relation to the painting. This can last 10–15 minutes or so and allows time for the students to respond and 'warms' up the sensory nerve endings in the skin
2. Fabric explorations of the painting moving on to other sensory explorations, sound, smell using the velvet wrap and the lace collar – portrait of students using a gilt/highly decorative frame
3. A baroque dance to music
4. Close with the facial exploration using soft brushes in relation to the painting

A bespoke sensory resource: the heavy velvet wrap

A physical extension of the painting. The velvet wrap would be a vehicle to experience a variety of sensory entry points into the Frans Hals painting. It would allow for:

- **Wrapping and draping** around students so that they can experience the velvet texture of the clothing depicted in the painting and in a similar fashion to the cavalier
- **Pockets** that could support a number of experiences. They could have weights so that they accentuate the 'heaviness' of the fabric, smells that refer to trade such as cloves or frankincense. They could contain coins that jangled
- **Buttons** – oversized, different materials such as metal or wood that could enhance the tactile experience

    * Sequence of exploration: it would be wise to focus on one aspect/sensory pathway at a time so that students don't find it too overwhelming.

Improvisation of light in the space

Using the light and dark, windows and lights/torches in the classroom – this can also be a point of enquiry. Moving between light and dark several times and watching the student's responses to inform how this could develop.

The National Trust

The National Trust was founded in 1895 with the aim to preserve historical and natural places and to make them accessible for all to enjoy. The National Trust is responsible for over 780 miles of coastline and has more than 250,000 hectares of land with over 500 historic houses, castles, parks, and gardens and is the custodian of over a million works of art. The National Trust is a significant player within the cultural fabric of England.

The interview

The interview covers three broad themes within inclusion: access, participation, and representation. Key points have been extracted in how the National Trust is increasing its inclusive practices.

Interview with Tiger de Souza, people engagement director at National Trust

Engaging in conversations

'Engaging conversations across all spaces with a range of identities and challenges and through an intersectional lens, we are all intersectional. Underrepresented and minorities – all together are the majority, challenging the notion of differences. These things impact on as part of our identity, we need to think inclusively not exclusively, be willing to be open and respond, because we all benefit'.

Systemic change

'Holistic and systemic change is challenging. Thinking about a range of barriers and looking at other places/spaces allyship and not thinking in specific identities. We think all allies and people have complex identities and different needs; we are developing a broad understanding of inclusion'.

Model of inclusive development

'The National Trust is accelerating a model of development in e-learning to support staff and volunteers and developing a policy position and action plan for the next ten years. The Trust is also actively posing questions: how do we do translate policy into practical actions – intent and activity?'

Practical change

'The National Trust has made significant multimillion-pound investment into its infrastructure. One strand is the effective planning for inclusion by developing accessible changing places toilet and the Trust is carrying out audits; know what the provision is, what things are in place, up-skill people where needed'.
   * Changing Places is a British consortium and campaign which aims to improve accessible toilet facilities. It maintains a list of toilets which meet its requirements.

Partnerships

'The National Trust has partnered with organisations. It currently has a pilot with Royal National Institute of the Blind and using new technology; magic table 360 to support inclusion and has partners with local disability groups to support a local inclusive offer. The trust also has a broad statement on its commitment to inclusion'.

Acting on feedback

Tiger describes this as a 'constant conversation, open and receptive and openly curious, developing a more inclusive mind set'. And gives the example: 'Visitor information such as Roman baths have developed easy feedback mechanism by offering paper and pencil at all communication points. This approach is low cost and low tech – promoting visitor engagement and building credibility. This easy to do approach to problem solving is easy to do and builds confidence'.

Curating different histories

'The National Trust has curated different histories and narratives, such as women in power, legacy of colonialism and slavery and is engaged in exploring a wider range of histories to include those whose stories haven't been told'.

A reflective approach to change

'The inclusion team is small; however, the director general is committed to inclusion. It's a priority target post pandemic. The curatorial team appeals to and support distinct audiences and are reflective, listening, open, and learning'.

Young people

'The development of young people hubs are informing this aspect of the National Trust's development and supporting them in engaging with a new audience. Parents are the gatekeepers to the National Trust. The Trust has been developing play areas and play spaces to support that direct relationship with the outdoors and natural history/natural heritages. The National Trust are custodians of natural beauty and history. Octavia Hill, one of the founders of the National Trust, started with outdoor spaces and was an early inclusionist, working in social housing in London where she championed access to fresh air and the countryside. This belief inspired the National Trust; this still holds true today and inclusion is a formative driver in their development going forward'.

Progress within inclusion

'Developing access plans that show progression from bronze, silver, and gold. The foundation stages create the culture and increase accessibility and as they progress it becomes more sustainable, and more embedded within the culture. The plans enabling National Trust venues to have a road map and to make investment at the right time with a clear direction of travel and trajectory of change. Evaluating progress helps to increase the rate of change and supports sustainable and strategic change'.

Allyship

'The National Trust has a philosophy to openly share their challenges and their journey and to work within the sector of arts and culture so that all benefit from their experiences and learning. To replicate success and to learn in the spirit of openness and allyship'.

Developed a collegiate nature towards problem solving to increase inclusion

Tiger describes the importance of engaging both audiences that are not engaging with the National Trust alongside those that are engaged as '83% of people acquire a disability in their lifetime'. He describes the interventions that are designed for specific and pre-existing audiences such as those with dementia; developing sloped access also benefits a wide range of other audiences, such as those with push chairs and visual impairment.

Summary of key points

- Place inclusion centrally within your work/mission
- Broad concept of inclusion; intersectional to meet the broadest needs
- Look at other institutions to support your development
- Partner with organisations strategically to increase inclusion
- Become curious
- Be open and receptive to conversations and change
- Think of quick, low-cost, and accessible solutions that can be put in place quickly as a response
- Audit and be strategic, think practical and attitudinal
- Develop structural hubs/organisations to access wider audiences
- Develop plans that show progress so that change is cultural and sustainable
- Work collectively in the space to increase inclusion and work in the spirit of allyship

---

Concluding notes

As explored in chapter 8, the impact of co-production cannot be underestimated. In both of these case studies the impact for students, schools, and the cultural organisation was made clear. There was greater impact for the students, and much more enjoyable and meaningful activities were constructed. There was legacy in both cultural institutions and the schools in terms of resources developed and an understanding of how to develop programmes that are both inclusive in their delivery and design.

12 Relaxed performances and venues

This chapter explores the concept of a relaxed performance in two different cultural organisations: Battersea Arts Centre and the English National Opera (ENO). It looks at how these organisations have taken two different approaches. Battersea Arts has been guided by Jess Thom of Touretteshero on their journey towards becoming a relaxed venue, and the ENO are at a point of strategic change and have adopted an ambitious five-year strategy placing relaxed performances centrally within this. This chapter contains an interview with Jess to understand the approach and her personal politics within this space and an interview with Amy and Beth from the ENO.

How to use this chapter

Through interviews key points are drawn out so that the relaxed performance approach is understood and articulated effectively, describing how these performances are planned and practically delivered and supported. The chapter unpacks the approach to understand what it means in practice and the future implications within the cultural sector.

Implications for schools

At the end of the chapter are key points that are useful for schools to consider in supporting them in becoming relaxed venues.

Jess Thom and Battersea Arts Centre

Jess Thom is a theatre-maker and comedian who established Touretteshero, an alter ego and project aimed at increasing awareness of Tourette syndrome. Jess is an activist in the space of arts, culture, and inclusion and has adopted the social model of inclusion to inform her work. More information and how to contact Jess can be found at the end of the chapter.

Jess Thom

'When we talk about inclusive practice at its most basic, what we're talking about is the difference between assuming everyone does things exactly the same way, and then finding that we will do things differently. It's not news that our bodies and minds work in different ways. We've known that for generations, but we continue to promote the idea that there's one valid way of engaging with the world'.

The interview

The interview is organised under subheadings and discusses Jess's approach to her work in this space by initially exploring her personal politics and how this has informed her work. It goes on to outline how Jess uses the social model of inclusion to look for solutions to barriers and how this has guided her work with Battersea Arts Centre.

A lived experiences of barriers

'I identify as a disabled person because I experience barriers in the world. I'm quite happy to say that I have Tourette syndrome, which is one of the impairments that I have. And when I say impairment, these are facts about my body so I'm someone who has Tourette syndrome, and I'm dyslexic, and I experienced pain and fatigue. Disability is the lived experience of barriers because of how the world is structured and set up.

DOI: 10.4324/9781003122258-12

'Those are the facts, the reality of my body. That's my individual reality. All our bodies and minds work in different ways, my body works in a particular way. Disability for me means being prevented from functioning by the way that society is structured'.

Identity-first language and self-labelling

'I use identity-first language, so I say disabled person rather than the person with a disability as I feel that it fits better with the social model of disability, so disability isn't me it's not something that I carry around with me as I'm more or less disabled in different settings depending on how thoughtfully and inclusively, they've been set up'.

Disability as a social construct

'The thing that does needs to change is society, to create more accessible and non-disabling spaces systems and attitudes'.

Battersea Arts Centre

Battersea Arts Centre was founded in 1974 in London. The Arts Centre has a community focus and uses the arts for creative change and to make connections and forge relationships. Battersea Arts Centre describes itself as a creative hub. In 2020 Battersea Arts Centre launched themselves as the first relaxed venue in the world. They have been guided on this journey by Jess Thom, who has designed the approach outlined in the following interview. The journey was supported by Arts Council England's Change Makers programme.

> 'A relaxed approach offers a warm and radical Welcome to people who might have historically been excluded by the traditional rules of etiquette'.
>
> Jess Thom

The seven key elements of relaxed performance

1. A shared understanding about what a relaxed performance is
2. Information is available ahead of a show that uses words and pictures as preshow information so that you can understand what to expect
3. Staff have received disability equality training and take an inclusive approach
4. An announcement at the start of the show acknowledges that it's a relaxed performance and gives everyone the freedom to move and make noise and go in and out as needed
5. Chill-out spaces are provided that are external to the performance space that people can go to if they need to take a break
6. A multisensory approach is taken, thinking about the sensory landscape, adapting this if required, and communicating that to the audience
7. Finally, a plan is formulated for what to do if anyone makes a complaint about someone and how to manage this

Removal of labour

'Embed these as something that's part of every programme with the aims to take labour away from disabled people'.

Cultural curation

Cultural curation is what happens around what is and isn't made accessible to disabled people.

What is made accessible?

'At the moment, the model for relaxed performances and other types of accessible performance is that fundamentally venues choose which performance they make accessible. That means that disabled people, people who have specific access requirements, don't have access to the same range of cultural opportunities'.

A methodology of change: three key principles

We ask the relaxed venue to adopt three key principle commitments; however, we understand that they might inherit some physical or systemic barriers that take time and investment to undo.

1. **No new barriers**
   In the first instance no new barriers means thinking about a diversity of bodies and minds. If you're making something or setting something up, whether that's creating a new show or laying out the tables in a cafe, think about a range of bodies, minds, and perspectives, and that you are **not creating any new barriers**.

2. **Quality of experience**
   The second commitment is a quality of experience. Sometimes it feels as if disabled people can technically access something that's good enough, **that commitment is not good enough** for something to be just technically accessible, there needs to be a quality of experience too. That doesn't mean that people have to do things in exactly the same way, but it does mean that if you are adding audio, make sure that the audio description is thought about and invested in, in the same way as the visual aesthetic of the show. If there is captioning, then it is thought about creatively. If a wheelchair user is taking a route through a performance, then make sure that it is of equal quality to any other audience member's experience.

3. **Reduce bias**
   The final commitment is to **reduce bias** and to acknowledge the accumulative impact of the message that our environments send us all the time. Traditionally, lots of venues and particularly theatres might have sent messages to disabled people that you're not thought about. You're not welcome, you're a fire risk, you're an afterthought.

Embedding access

Perceptual barriers

'They're not always even real walls but sometimes the perceptions of how you behave and respond in a space is a barrier in itself'.

Reducing negative messages

'By embedding access confidently and reducing bias, so that you know where the accessible toilet is, you know where the hearing loop is, by making sure these things are thought about and competently provided, you can reduce the impact of those negative messages that people are being sent, and instead they're sent messages that they are thought about, valued, and welcome'.

An ongoing process

'Relaxed venues are an ongoing process, they're not a sort of status that you achieve, that you reach, and that you never have to do any work. Being a relaxed venue is the process of constantly identifying and removing disabling barriers and promoting and advocating for disability culture'.

Structural change

'The relaxed approach needs to go across every part of the programming, and also every level of the organisation. That type of deep-rooted change obviously takes time; it's not a perfect process. It is about having clear commitments, clear targets and ambitions and being open to adapt. Open to conversations and a dialogue to continually prioritising getting as close to right as you can'.

Expertise and the long-term view

'Also recognise that there needs to be someone who has specific expertise who is championing good practice within the organisation and who people could go to when they have questions. Someone at a senior level to help guide and shape change because it's an evolving process. making sure that it is representative of the ambition, to include and represent disability culture at every level'.

Future

'Seeing how it works in different contexts is good because part of the ambition for relaxed venues was not just thinking about theatres or performance spaces but also thinking about museums and galleries and other public spaces'.

English National Opera

Founded in 1931 by Lillian Baylis, the English National Opera (ENO) was known at that time as the Sadler's Wells Opera Company. It took the radical decision to sing established operas in English and to make opera accessible through affordable prices.

How to use this information

This gives you some insights into how these are part of a cultural shift at the ENO, how this is part of a wider strategic approach to relaxed performances. How the relaxed performances have evolved and how they are leveraging change across the whole of ENO's approach to inclusion.

> 'The ENO is the national opera house for everyone. We were founded on the principle that we are open and accessible to anyone, whoever they are'.
>
> (Taken from ENO's *Commitment to Inclusivity & Relevance*.)

Engage

> 'ENO Engage exists to open up new possibilities for opera in people's lives. By turning the artform sideways, upside down and inside out, we reinvent it as a tool for social impact and change'.
>
> (Taken from ENO's *Strategic Plan 2022–27*.)

Engage is ENO's strategy to use opera as a vehicle for positive and meaningful impact in society, exploring how it can be used across a number of places and spaces such as health trusts and schools and to forge new partnerships.

The interview

The interview was with Amy Powell, Programme Manager, ENO Engage, and Beth Warnock, Head of Department, ENO Engage.

The interview took place after their programming was paused due to the pandemic. This pause also meant that their remit changed, and with their innovative 'Breathe' programme they responded to Long Covid. This has acted as a catalyst to consider opera in the widest possible sense – its relevance, its ability to engage and be creative and to consider not only its creative and cultural relevance but also the social impact that opera can have.

Leadership

The influence of inclusion on leadership and decision making is at board level and is structural to the ENO. This has given equality, diversity, and inclusion (EDI) a broader, more holistic remit within the ENO and a voice at a strategic level.

Opera as a creative space

ENO is challenging itself; opera is often perceived as an elite art form to be broken down, explored, and played with in the spirit or creativity; re-staged, re-purposed, changed, and updated . . . what are the creative possibilities that opera has?

> 'We do this by delivering immersive, playful programmes that surprise, inspire and connect people'."
>
> (Taken from ENO's *Strategic Plan 2022–27*.)

Interrogating what opera can be

Beth: 'Convince me, I'm taking the position that opera needs to be made relevant and made real' and 'Challenging the organisations expectations of what opera is, and what it can be'.

Both Beth and Amy are framing the organisation's practices within a questioning dialogue as a means to unpack and understand the creative and inclusive potential that opera can have. This approach is driven by the need to be relevant to contemporary audiences and wider society more generally.

Relaxed performances

The first relaxed performance was *The Mikado* in 2019 and was led by the artistic team. There has been a recent restructure and the relaxed performances are now led by the education team.

The first performance was attended by 400 people and was supported by Mousetrap Theatre projects. The response to the performance was overwhelmingly positive and gave insights into how opera could be experienced differently and the creative scope that this gave. This coincided with the restructure of the ENO, where relaxed performances are now part of a strategic approach to inclusion. They have subsequently performed *HMS Pinafore* as a relaxed performance. *The Cunning Little Vixen* is the ENO's latest offering.

Mousetrap Theatre Projects

Based in the West End, Mousetrap Theatre Education Charity is dedicated to enriching the lives of young people and making theatre accessible.

Characteristics of a relaxed performance

Beth and Amy describe the established 'norms' and the perception of how an opera 'should' be experienced as a barrier. The relaxed performances are allowing the ENO to explore, consider, and reconceptualise the creative spaces around opera performances. The relaxed performances are now part of a device to show how opera can be experienced to the wider ENO organisation as part of their strategy for change organisationally.

Inclusion in the broadest terms

> "Inclusive, rather than exclusive to those who need it'.

The driver for the performances is to be inclusive within the broadest sense: age, D/deaf, disabled, neurodivergent . . . inclusive of all who might want to attend opera in a different way. Beth describes how she brought her 96-year-old grandfather, as he felt confident and reassured by the relaxed arrangements.

Behaviours

There are historic conventions of how opera is to be experienced. This isn't the case during a relaxed performance. Active participation and responses are encouraged, and this is facilitated by one of the lead performers. It breaks with the usual opera conventions, welcoming the audience from the stage and introducing the conductor, who brings attention to the sheer scale of the orchestra and the musicians.

Demystifying the mechanics of opera

Part of the introduction is to 'demystify' opera and to signpost moments in the performance to where people are actively encouraged to participate and to 'introduce all the musicians in a relaxed and playful manner'. Here all people are acknowledged and actively included – the performers, the audience, and the musicians. This playful introduction sets the tone and the 'relaxed expectations'. People are encouraged to go and watch the musicians in action during the performance. This aspect of the relaxed performance is something that the ENO is keen to explore further by filming the pit and the orchestra and making this part of a holistic opera experience.

Anticipation of need

Prior to the performance, points that might be problematic are identified and signposted, so that they can be mitigated. The audience are informed of these as part of the materials they receive prior to the performance.

Resources sent prior to the performance are

- Visual story
- Timetable
- Sonic story for the performance.
- A short video was also made available that outlined what to expect at an ENO relaxed performance.

Post-performance evaluations

Information is gathered post performance through questionnaires, and this helps to inform next steps, responding to the audience as an equitable partner in this journey towards increasing inclusion at the ENO.

The experience

The welcome from the point of arrival frames the experience as relaxed. Props and costumes are displayed as you arrive so that the sensory qualities can be seen, explored, and handled alongside crafting activities. ★ This was also accompanied by a performer, but due to Covid this hasn't been possible.

During the performance

People can communicate freely and use any tech that they need such as phones and iPads. Beth describes how these devices are often essential for communication and that to not have them can induce anxiety and stress and that 'turning life isn't possible'. People can also eat and drink during the performance.

Chill-out spaces

Chill-out spaces at present are informal areas away from the auditorium where you can still access the performance digitally, but allows you time away or another way of experiencing the performance altogether.

Future partnership and co-production

There are plans to consider the creative opportunities that the chill-out spaces present. These could have elements that draw on the creative focus of the ENO – voice, costume, and design. The ENO wants to engage local community partners to co-produce these spaces. Here the ENO are moving to a point of structural inclusion through the development of these partnerships. The community partnerships will also offer further opportunities for inclusion to be embedded through mechanisms such as sounding boards, and this supports the long-term, five-year inclusive strategy that the ENO has developed.

Relaxed performances as a vehicle for change

The relaxed performances bring a faster rate of change as they offer concrete evidence of the impact of these performances and the possibilities of greater inclusion and the creative space this offers. Like the National Trust, ENO's founders were radicals of their time. The ENO are re-engaging with the spirit of this mission with a drive to make opera relevant and inclusive to contemporary audiences.

Creative conversations

Amy and Beth are engaging in creative conversations around the performances and how they might be reimagined to engage a more diverse audience, become more inclusive, and retain and extend their creativity through this process.

The goal is to acknowledge the 'whole' opera experience as a starting point and develop this through a holistic and organisational conversation inclusive of all those involved in the production but with a clear remit around inclusion to guide, support, and steer the conversation.

They consider:

- Length of time of the opera
- What is appropriate, what can be cut down (curate the experience)

Moving forward

Amy and Beth are determined to use some of their headliners, iconic operas, to send a message and to promote their long-term commitment to inclusion.

ENO, identity, and inclusion

The ENO is articulating their identity, who they are and that they want you to come. They are interrogating, considering, and reconceptualising opera as a point of creative exploration.

Digital inclusion

Website and digital inclusion are on the agenda, particularly around booking arrangements: 'booking shouldn't be difficult'. Beth describes how she is constantly investigating how to reduce labour so that there is equity and that everyone has the same experience when booking a ticket.

Mapping: physical inclusion and access

It is important to map the physical journeys to the opera from transport hubs, considering wheelchairs, buggies, steps between places, and places to sit. Consider the possibilities for seating within the auditorium so that wheelchairs are fully included and considered and not separate.

Implications for schools

- Communication with visitors/parents on what to expect/expectations of a school's performance or event to ensure that the school is being inclusive of the wider school community
- Guidance around relaxed events to ensure common understanding and that people feel welcome
- Consider the creative opportunities of events and reimagining performances
- Consider digital inclusion: are websites inclusive of the wider community, is there any labour that can be reduced in accessing information?

Concluding notes

It is evident that there is a lot of potential in using a relaxed framework in progressing inclusion and inclusive practices. Both the Battersea Arts Centre and the English National Opera have consciously engaged with a model that questions accepted orthodoxies to become more inclusive. This approach gives space for growth and increases social impact, but also importantly it acknowledges the creative opportunities and potential that the relaxed approach has.

Contact details

Jess Thom
Touretteshero
www.touretteshero.com

13 Where next in art, culture, and inclusion?

This is the final chapter in the book, and it poses the question: where next for art, culture, and inclusion?

This chapter looks at some of the common themes explored in the book and how these have increased access, representation, and participation in arts and culture. It describes some of the key mechanisms to support this, and it considers the long-term view in this space and how we can make it sustainable. And finally, where next for schools and cultural organisations?

The chapter is broken down into key headings with key points listed under each of the headings:

1. **Common themes**
2. **Innovation, creativity and inclusion**
3. **Characteristics of a culturally inclusive school, a conversation with Queensmill School**
4. **Structural, sustainable, and practical inclusion: how to achieve this?**
5. **IVE Bridge, Humber and Yorkshire, inclusion, and diversity lab: Interview with Sarah Mumford**
6. **Connections and allyship: getting connected and opportunities to share**
7. **Long-term view and agents of change, the Cultural Inclusion Manifesto**

Common themes

Relationships

Invest in relationships. Consider this within the widest sense of community with the school located at the centre. Consider your local identity, your place-based identity. Find out who is in your local area and how you can work together to increase your impact and look for opportunities for joint working.

Co-production

Co-production and collective working across education and with your cultural partners increases impact and understanding and can be transformational across both spaces. Make time to develop an understanding of how you can work well together. Map opportunities where you can work together.

Innovation, creativity, and inclusion

A transformative pedagogy

There is an emerging new discourse in education which is inclusive, anti-ableist, and transformative. Chapter 8 on anti-ableist pedagogy describes this and outlines some of the characteristics of this pedagogy. There is more here to unpack and to understand, but there is huge scope here. There is the potential to consider and articulate how creativity can be encouraged and nurtured, how learning can be co-constructed and guided, and how through this process all people are 'seen' and their personhood acknowledged. This type of pedagogy and pedagogical understanding spans schools and cultural organisations and truly brings people together to learn in equitable relationships focused on empowerment and the learning journey.

A creative approach

Through working with artist practitioners unburdened by the structures of teaching which in themselves can be barriers, a creative approach was co-produced. Creativity and inclusion and the possibility of new and different ways of doing were explored, ones that are inclusive of different bodies and minds. Here, exploring artwork or concepts through the lenses of the students gave them new life. Culture isn't something that should be preserved in aspic to

DOI: 10.4324/9781003122258-13

be seen from afar and revered. In chapter 11 on heritage settings paintings were made real, new interpretations were made, and the students made connections. Paintings became alive, transcending time to be present in the classroom through the immediacy of touch. I think there's real poetry here, the ability to focus in, slow down, and bring paintings alive through sensory exploration. This isn't only happening in the classroom. Cultural institutions such as the English National Opera are thinking radically about their art forms, and there are boundless opportunities for other institutions to follow suit.

Defining creativity

The book outlines how this can be achieved. Building on the pre-existing work of Sir Ken Robinson, we use a narrative approach to describe creativity and learning so that both can be acknowledged and built upon.

Characteristics of a culturally inclusive school, a conversation with Queensmill School

Queensmill School is a large school in West London that supports students with autistic spectrum disorder from reception to 19 and is part of an academy. The conversation was with the following:

- Aymeline Bell, a member of the school's senior leadership team
- Elise Robinson, their creative arts lead
- Lisha Rooney, a parent of one of their students

We discussed how schools are culturally inclusive and through this discussion I pulled together the characteristics in the following boxed sections.

Characteristics of the parental school dynamic

- Schools engage with the parental view and held conversations that support co-production and allied problem solving
- Schools co-produced with parents, listening to, responding to, and being involved in the curriculum, and this leads to benefits beyond the school
- Schools see themselves as gatekeepers to society, preparing young people for society and also advocacy within society
- Schools emphasise parental partnerships
- Schools work within a framework of equity/equality of opportunity

Leadership qualities in school

- Leadership supports challenging and progressive pedagogy
- Leadership is confident and empowering within the school's culture, supporting and encouraging teachers to take creative risks
- Leadership acknowledges that these activities and initiatives are complex and offers support and encouragement
- Leadership values progressive practice, understanding the complexity of this, and makes space and time to reassure
- Leadership challenges expectations, both internal and external, in terms of both access and representation
- Leadership poses questions, challenging norms and orthodoxy around creativity and practice
- Leadership ensures that students have access to a range of high-quality creative arts activities through dedicated, creative art teachers
- Leadership in school supports the student's voice within the creative process
- Leadership affirms creative outcomes by celebrating them in the school and school culture
- Leadership promotes visibility of students by being 'seen' and valued within initiatives
- Leadership promotes artists and role models who describe themselves as D/deaf, disabled, and neurodivergent

Characteristics of partnership working

- Partnership working promotes long-term, sustainable relationships
- Partnership working is developed through co-production
- Partnership working builds rapport and relationship through professional dialogue

---

- Partnership working identifies opportunities through practical working
- Partnership working promotes cultural inclusion in this space
- Partnership working leads to cultural change in both spaces
- Partnership working challenges stereotypes
- Partnership working considers notions of citizenship and personhood and realises these
- Partnership working promotes real and relevant representation that is authentic

Structural, sustainable, and practical inclusion: how to achieve this?

Build community

Build community and acknowledge that we all have a role – schools, families, and cultural partners.

Make inclusion part of the culture

Adopt systems that aren't additional but are strategic. Embed systems and approaches ranging from pedagogy to co-production. Describe its characteristics and have a shared common understanding.

Work strategically with partners

Build time for professional conversations to take place and make sure that this becomes practice. Map opportunities and build on this, seeing where you can bring value by working collectively. See partnership working as long term and see how you can support each other's learning in this space. Give language to what you are doing so that it can be understood and scaled up.

Understand inclusion and inclusive practices

Understanding that inclusion and inclusive practices are constantly being rewritten. They have to be revisited and made structural and part of the practice.

Funding and funders

Make connections with funders. It takes time to develop a case for support, to understand the need and how best to address this. Talk to funders, make connections, and build rapport. Identify whom you might work with and approach them, but be mindful that all these things take time.

Time

Realise that there is a time commitment to sustaining inclusion. Build it into systems and acknowledge that sometimes it takes time to get to know people, move to action, and see impact in relationships, in co-production, and in the co-construction of learning. But rest assured that given time your impact will be greater, the learning deeper, and the enjoyment greater.

IVE Bridge, Humber and Yorkshire, inclusion, and diversity lab

Interview with Sarah Mumford

I interviewed Sarah Mumford, the programme director of IVE Bridge Humber and Yorkshire (bridge organisations are set up by the Arts Council and are designed to connect the cultural sector and the education sector and support young people's access to the arts), to understand how they had approached this work through their inclusion and diversity labs. The inclusion and diversity labs were born out of their work in this space and their work as a response to the *Creative Case for Arts* (2016). This is a project that was initially piloted internally and has subsequently developed into a training programme that can affect long-term transformational change within organisations. IVE uses case studies to demonstrate how the training can support this change. The following diagram outlines this process of change.

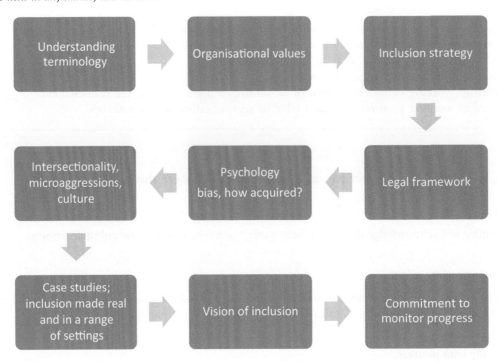

Connections and allyship: getting connected and opportunities to share

Connections and networks

Make connections within your school and within your community. Join networks, ask questions, and be curious about others. Talk actively about how and in what ways you might work together to increase impact and awareness of inclusion and inclusive practices.

Allyship

See inclusion in the broadest terms and how it can benefit all; see people who work in this space as allies and describe them as such.

Long-term view and agents of change, the Cultural Inclusion Manifesto

The Cultural Inclusion Manifesto (CIM) was co-authored by myself and Rachael Christophides. The CIM is a relatively new network. It works across individuals, schools, cultural organisations, families, artists, and politicians for real and sustainable change. It works to increase access, participation, and representation in arts and culture for disabled children and young people.

It asserts that we can and must do better. It calls on all those involved within this space to commit to greater cultural inclusion for people with special educational needs and disabilities. It calls on schools and policy makers and all those agencies involved in the creation, funding, and promotion of arts and culture to commit cultural inclusion, not only in spirit but practically through policy, strategy, and implementation in order to achieve lasting and sustainable change.

It hosts conferences and develops initiatives based on identified needs and amplifies good practice. In part, one of the reasons I was asked to write this book was because of my activism in arts, culture, and inclusion. I am incredibly proud of the CIM, and I urge all readers to sign up to the manifesto, to collectively own the manifesto and be part of this movement for greater inclusion in the space of arts and culture.

Concluding notes: where next?

The book has unpacked some of the broad themes within arts, culture, and inclusion, but there is more work to be done. There are some very exciting areas to explore: new inclusive pedagogies and the space where inclusion and creativity meets offers new cultural opportunities. New ways of doing, being, seeing, and experiencing all need to be navigated, mapped, and articulated so that these practices can be shared and amplified.

Glossary

Ableism Describes discriminatory behaviours that favour non-disabled people.

Assessment A measurement of learning.

Baseline An initial assessment that is made and then used to measure against.

British Values The four British Values are democracy, the rule of law, individual liberty, and mutual respect for and tolerance of those with different faiths and beliefs and for those without faith.

Broad and balanced curriculum A curriculum that provides a wide range of opportunities for pupils to learn.

Case study The process and recording of research into the development of a specific person, group, or situation over a period of time.

Co-constructed learning A collaborative process in which learners (students and teachers) learn from one another to build and expand their knowledge based on one another's ideas and contributions.

Critical pedagogy Teaching that critiques and questions structures of power and oppression.

Cultural capital Refers to the level of accumulated knowledge, behaviours, and skills that a student uses and that demonstrates their cultural awareness and knowledge.

Curriculum Refers to a body of skills and knowledge.

Disablism The discrimination towards and oppression of disabled people.

Disability-focused organisation An organisation whose work is focused on people who are disabled.

Disability-led organisation An organisation that is led by disabled people.

Education, Health and Care plans Legal documents outlining the support a child or young person will receive to meet their special needs across education, health, and social care.

Engagement Level of interest and curiosity that a student demonstrates in an activity. The Department for Education defines five areas of engagement: exploration, realisation, anticipation, persistence, and initiation.

Entry point The point of entry into a subject and/or curriculum for a student(s).

Inclusion The acts, systems, and structures of including people.

Labelling A signposting exercise that can give you some understanding of the impairment that people have and what barriers this could lead to. Labels do not define, and it's person first, label second. It is important to remember that labels are only used if they are empowering and enabling.

Learning objective The expected learning within a lesson scheme of work or activity.

Medical model of disability Locates the disability within the individual and that they need to be 'fixed' in order to access and participate in society.

Multifaceted entry points The number of identified entry points into a subject and/or curriculum for a wide range of student(s).

Neurodivergent Differing in neurological or mental function from what is considered typical or normal (frequently used with reference to autistic spectrum condition); not neurotypical.

Neurodiversity The range of differences in neurological or mental function that is regarded as part of the normal variation in the human population.

Normalcy The narrative around what is considered 'normal' and 'expected', especially around bodies and minds and their abilities; this influences how disabled people are treated and perceived.

Othering Describes an individual or a group of individuals as different, separate from another group.

Phenomenology The study of individuals' lived experience of the world, their subjective experience.

Person centred Placing the student, their needs, and their aspirations centrally within their learning.

Personhood The quality or condition of being seen and acknowledged as an individual person.

Qualitative assessment Assessment that is descriptive in nature.

Quantitative assessment Assessment that uses numbers and percentages to show learning and is often associated with externalised criteria.

Scheme of work Outlines the expected learning to be covered over a given period of time.

SEND code of practice Statutory guidance for organisations that work with and support children and young people with special educational needs.

SMSC   SMSC stands for spiritual, moral, social, and cultural development.

Social model of disability   Locates the barriers within the structure and systems of society and seeks to reveal them so that they can be removed or mitigated. Opposite to the medical model of disability.

Social role valorisation and normalisation   A model that acknowledges the power of how people are portrayed and its subsequent impact on the value that society locates within that individual.

Student voice   Describes the mechanisms of how students are active participants in their learning and how they are able to influence the decisions that inform this.

Index

For Product Safety Concerns and Information please contact our EU
representative GPSR@taylorandfrancis.com Taylor & Francis Verlag GmbH,
Kaufingerstraße 24, 80331 München, Germany

Printed and bound by CPI Group (UK) Ltd, Croydon, CR0 4YY
08/06/2025
01897012-0004